whitefella
wandering

Whitefella Wandering is an engrossing story of a personal journey through contemporary landscapes and cultures, both physical and spiritual. Phil Thomson takes us on his travels through Australian suburbia, remote Aboriginal communities and the highlands and islands of New Guinea; on a wander from whitefella knowledge and certainty to wonder at other ways of seeing, understanding and knowing.

The universe laughs at our attempts to define it in merely western scientific terms. Ours is the only culture that is committed entirely to the physical as an explanation for everything. All other cultures, vanished and surviving, have enriched their physical sciences with an understanding of the spiritual world. I believe it is a mark of our arrogance that we disregard all other human constructs of the universe … Such a dismissive gaze overturns all the ways we humans have learned to live with each other over the millennia.

Phil Thomson's *Whitefella Wandering* delights in the unexpected, embraces uncertainty, celebrates difference.

whitefella
wandering

Phil Thomson

FREMANTLE ARTS CENTRE PRESS

First published 2001 by
FREMANTLE ARTS CENTRE PRESS
25 Quarry Street, Fremantle
(PO Box 158, North Fremantle 6159)
Western Australia.
www.facp.iinet.net.au

Consultant Editor Janet Blagg.
Production Coordinator Cate Sutherland.
Cover Designer Becky Chilcott.

Typeset by Fremantle Arts Centre Press
and printed by Success Print.

National Library of Australia
Cataloguing-in-publication data

Thomson, Phil, 1953– .
    Whitefella Wandering.

    ISBN 1 86368 316 X.

    1. Thomson, Phil, 1953– — Journeys — Papua New Guinea —
    Biography. 2. Thomson, Phil, 1953– — Journeys — India — Biography.
    3. Thomson, Phil, 1953– — Journeys — Australia — Biography.
    4. Spiritual biography — Australia. 5. Aborigines, Australian — Social
    life and customs. 6. Culture. 7. Australia — Description and travel.
    8. Papua New Guinea — Description and travel.
    9. India — Description and travel. I. Title.

920.094

The State of Western Australia has made an investment in this project
through ArtsWA in association with the Lotteries Commission.

Publication of this title was assisted by the Commonwealth Government
through the Australia Council, its arts funding and advisory body.

To my kids,
Ren and Nina,
and to all things wild

Acknowledgements

As this story is, in essence, a true one I have encouraged those people who appear within to read it before publication. I have deleted or changed passages that were of concern. Where requested, and in cases where I could not ask permission, I have distorted the truth of names and places to avoid offence.

I thank everyone who has allowed me to share these stories, especially: my family, Ren, Nina, Lynn, John, Mac and Marian; the Doiki family, Launi, Pauline and the people of Massiafaluka; my blackfella colleagues, Paul, Kelton, Ningali, Shorty, Theo, Franklin and Monty (Australia), and Simon, Samual, Moyang and Lina (Papua New Guinea); Daksha Sheth, her family and company; the traditional owners of vast tracts of Australia and Papua New Guinea for permitting me to wander through their country.

I am indebted to the support and wisdom I received from my early readers (Sally, Magan, Polly and Wendy), from my publisher and my wonderful editor Janet. Thanks also to the Australia Council and ArtsWA for the funds that kept me alive whilst I alternately slumped and tap-danced across my keyboard.

Contents

When I am with Aboriginal friends or colleagues we use the terms whitefella and blackfella freely to describe each other. They have other terms, of course, for the white devils who invaded their land. The Koories of the southern east coast call us Gubba — a shortening and blackening of the term 'government man'. In Papua New Guinea young kids and old people often call us Masta. I hated that when I first heard it, deeply shamed by the enforced servitude the name conjured. I grew a little more comfortable on realising Masta has lost its connotation of slavery and merely become a word for white man. We have become so ubiquitous that a term is needed to set us aside from the rest of the people of the world. Where I live, in the south of Western Australia, the Nyoongar people call us Wetjella — simply derived from the term whitefella. It seems to describe exactly what I am.

I am a whitefella, I am an Anglo-Celtic Australian male, and these attributes have affected my response to the strange events through which I have wandered, and coloured the way I describe and make sense of them.

My private relationships are not the business of this book and whilst my work as a theatre artist is often exciting to me I suspect it is of little interest to many readers. Thus you will not get a full picture of who I am. Without my family and my work you will only glimpse a small part of my disorderly life. This then is not a classical biography; it is more a series of encounters. Encounters by a whitefella with 'the other' — other ways of life, other ways of being. Often these have occurred in wild country, sometimes with wild people.

I am privileged to have been able to wander through wilderness populated by non-western cultures. I pray to all the gods that such mesmerising variety still exists at the start of the next millennium.

Quest

Music oozed from a knocked-about portable player as a few people danced in the dirt behind the bakery. I could see a sliver of moonlit ocean between the trees. An old man shuffled over towards me. I moved to one side to offer him a seat. He slowly lowered his bum to the concrete and leaned against the wall. He nodded a brief acknowledgement, then turned to watch the dancers without a word. I knew him to be Popeye PK, and I was glad he felt comfortable to sit with me.

We were the first white mob for many years to be invited to live at the north end of the 'mission'. We had come to perform a play, and were given a privileged opportunity to experience Aboriginal community life. Two of our company, cousins Paul and Mick, were Murri. They were indigenous to this place and had brought us home to stay with their people. We had a vague intention to try and stay relatively invisible and not disturb the locals. Instead, obvious if you think about it, we were an exotic attraction. We became unwitting hosts of a continuing party. Morning, noon and night visitors dropped in for a chat or a dance or a beer.

I had first seen Popeye PK the previous afternoon squashed between two other elders in the back of a beat up Ford. They had driven slowly through our audience, with a bouncy screech of noisy springs, just as our first show was about to begin. Carefully checking out the scene, with special attention to us, they cruised past and up the hill to stop with a gravel slide and a puff of dust. Everybody was looking at them. We held up the performance, in a muddled show of respect, waiting for them to get out of the car to watch the show. They didn't. They just sat and patiently waited for us to begin our story. The elders had come, but they had parked so far away they wouldn't hear a thing.

As the show got under way I climbed the dusty hillock to encourage the old men to move forward. Assuming they were staying back out of respect for our performance I assured them that we welcomed them closer.

'Nah, we'll be fine back here, son,' said the driver, who was the youngest elder. Popeye PK stared at me with great interest. And smiled when I left.

Throughout the hour-long show they sat in that hot car and watched us from a distance. We told a story of a lost Aboriginal boy and a homeless Martian youth; but the elders couldn't have been concerned with what we were actually saying as our words couldn't reach them. It was more as if they watched the patterns formed by the movements of excited kids and the physical language of the crowd. In some mysterious way they decided we were good for the community and gave us the thumbs up. From that point everyone made us completely welcome.

Now that he had sat beside me I felt confident in talking to Popeye.

'Did you enjoy the show?' I asked. He turned his head slowly to look at me. Brilliant white bristles punctured hard black skin around a black-lipped grin. He had the cloudy, watery eyes and gravelly slur of a man who likes his drinks and smokes.

'Yes,' he answered, but despite my questions was not interested in talking about our work, or about life in the community. He answered all of my questions with a grunt or a single word. He wasn't there to talk; he was there just for a laugh, of which he did a lot. He found the spectacle of the young men consistently failing to seduce the women of our troupe particularly funny.

Popeye stayed with us for several hours, saying little, drinking slowly, laughing. Eventually he got stiffly to his feet and shuffled across the yard — and to everyone's surprise began to rock his body to the beat of the music and dance. To his delight two of our actresses danced with him. He was not shy about a bit of body contact with the young women and chortled when they flirted with him.

Before he left that night he came to me and loudly offered to take our company to the sacred beach that he protected. He mentioned a magic healing pool and a cave that we should visit. When he talked everyone else was quiet, and when he left the whole party knew of the offer. The locals were impressed and a little amazed. Apparently few were given the privilege of visiting Popeye's beach, and none could remember whitefellas going.

It took weeks before the promise was realised. Popeye continued to hold out an invitation. He was most insistent, especially to me.

'You and me, we gotta go to that beach, to my beach.'

'Yes Popeye, whenever, please, yes, love to.'

He'd smile, and say tomorrow, or maybe next week, but he was always too charged up with cheap red wine to take us.

I was anxious to go — a trip to a sacred site with a real life elder in the tropical paradise of North Queensland. It was too good to miss and I began to plot with Paul and Mick. They were as anxious as I was to visit the old man's cave above the ocean waves. We hatched a plan. We kidnapped the ancient rascal.

By this time we had shifted out of the party madness of the mission settlement and into the bush. Having won acceptance from both the elders and Community Council we were allowed to reside in a beautiful timber and tin lean-to almost-house in the subtropical rainforest. Taking us out to our new home, the chairman of the community confided to me that we were the first white people allowed on that land in many years.

'Last ones out here were a couple of cops. They came out without permission. They left covered in bruises. Haven't had any unwanted visitors since.'

We found ourselves living in paradise. A creek bubbled alongside our hut and flowered vines wove themselves through the rafters. Here we were alone during the day, able to rehearse and come to terms with the new culture and environment within which we now lived. In the evenings our near neighbours would wander over with guitars and didgeridoo, and a roo tail or damper, and the glade would awaken.

So, according to our plan, we brought Popeye home for dinner, and asked visiting neighbours to leave their booze outside our boundaries. It was a lovely evening, warm and balmy with croaking frogs and muffled laughter. Occasionally Popeye decided it was time to go.

'I'll go home now,' he would say. 'You fellas can come and get me in the morning.'

'No, you stay here with us Uncle,' Paul would reply. 'It's good out here in the bush.' And the old man would look around, smile, and agree to stay. Until the thirst hit him again, when once more he tried to leave.

I was very happy. Sharing a fire with the joke-telling elder was a thrill. I knew that we were especially privileged to be going on a walk with this aging rogue, and I was excited. I had no inkling of the weird and wonderful experiences that were to come but I was already in the thrall of a new adventure unfolding in strange territory. The fire burnt down and the glow from a heap of hot embers marbled black and white faces with crimson highlights, and we relaxed with one another.

The peace was broken when in the distance we heard an engine racing, then the sounds of ripped gravel and a wounded clutch, drunken yells and brakes. Headlights flashed through blackness, illuminating giant leaves and startled faces. Our reverie was destroyed and we awaited the arrival of the marauding horde.

Five drunken men stormed into the clearing, blinking wildly in the firelight as they called for Paul. They were angry. As they pulled him away from us Paul calmed me by explaining they were his cousins who lived near town. He was in big trouble for not having visited them since he'd returned to the north.

'He's a stuck-up, coconut arsehole,' one cousin yelled in my face, 'and we've come to get him drunk.'

Coconut. A terrible insult to a sensitive blackfella. Dark on the outside, white in the core. I felt Paul stiffen. But he handled things well, thank the gods.

I went with him as we shepherded his mates, and their bottles, into the hut away from Popeye. I didn't think I'd be much help; I doubted they'd take kindly to a white stranger asking them not to drink. Paul managed somehow to calm things a little and explain what we were up to that evening.

'That's cool cuz,' declared Cousin One. 'We'll catch

some wild horses in the morning and ride over to the beach with yuz.'

But it wasn't cool. Gradually the drinking started, and Popeye was attracted. Then a mighty argument began between two of our visitors. It escalated violently in a mixture of local lingo, kriol and English obscenities, until the big bloke advanced threateningly on the smaller one, who suddenly drew a knife from his trouser band. With a blade flashing in his face the attacker grabbed a beer bottle and smashed the base off against a wall. They snarled and circled in the gloom. A feint, a lunge, the smell of fear. None of us said a word, nobody but the fighters moved. The big one moved in for the kill.

'No!' I screamed. It came from somewhere deep within me, without pre-thought or time for censor. The fighters froze, time stopped.

'Why the fuck are you doing this to one another?' I yelled. 'You Murris have got so much shit thrown at you, why do you take it out on each other? Why can't you work together instead of tearing each other to pieces? You make me sick!'

The guy with the bottle dropped it to the floor, the blade clattered alongside. We all breathed again. It seems miraculous, but within twenty minutes we were all lying like sardines between the walls, flaked out across three mattresses. Tightly packed and roughly covered we slept the sleep of the possessed, turning our bodies in unison.

The next morning our theatre troupe from the big city set off with Popeye into the rising sun. We left Paul behind to catch a wild brumby with his cousins and meet us at the beach. We walked for hours through rainforest and snake-infested grasslands. As Popeye walked, I noticed his back grow straighter and his eyes grow clear.

At the top of a rise I dislodged a small rock from the track and it tumbled down to the gully we'd just crossed. The old man turned and strode after it, picked it up and climbed slowly back up the hill. He carefully replaced the stone into its hole.

'We will leave things as we find them,' he instructed.

We could smell the sea for the final ten minutes as we climbed long sloping dunes through a lovely light scrub forest. Broaching the crest we stood panting, looking down from a high dune upon a perfect crescent of white sand and the infinite Pacific. Far out to sea lay the flat islands of the Barrier Reef whilst behind us rose jungle clad hills steaming clouds in the afternoon sun. We stood and marvelled at the wonder of it before plunging down the dunes and into the sea. Fish spun and darted through turquoise waters as we paddled our way up the beach to oyster covered rocks on the far side of a deep stream.

As he walked up the beach I realised how tall Popeye was, how straight his back, how clear his eyes. There was no doubting now the command of the man, nor the fact that he was home. He welcomed us to his land.

We were joined by another elder, another Popeye whose name I now forget. He'd been ferried over from the community in an aluminium runabout dinghy. His arrival posed a problem. The seas were getting up and the skipper was looking for volunteers to ride with him back to the community. He wanted to leave at once, and three of us were needed to hold down the prow as he crashed into the surf. Whoever went would have to beg a lift back to our campsite and retrace our journey to the beach. I was worried about Paul, and so volunteered, as did Mick who was also anxious about his cousin. Susie, who was a fanatical bushwalker as well as an actor, joined the party.

We raced through spray-laced winds, up and down the

silky curves of ocean swell and across angry gashes of rips and rough passage. The aluminium dinghy shook and twisted in the tidal forces. We would hang, time frozen, above grey-green troughs before spearing, laughing and yelling, through walls of foam.

At the community, we begged a lift from the Council Chairman and twenty minutes later we were back where we started at our bush cabin, with another long walk ahead of us. As the three of us started down the track we saw a crumpled bundle of limbs and clothes stacked against a tree. It was Paul. His head was grazed and his body bruised. And he was drunk.

He stirred as we approached and raved about being thrown twice from a saddle-less horse. He refused to come with us, sure he would soon catch a brumby which would allow him to ride, determined to find his cousins who had disappeared into the scrub. We protested; he was going to kill himself, or get lost, or fall asleep. He pulled away from our concerns and walked back up the track. I ran after him.

'We need you, you bastard,' I whispered forcefully into his ear. This was between him and me, and I didn't want the others to hear our exchange. It is not a good idea to censure young warriors in public. Their egos are fragile.

'This is your land, for Christ's sake. Popeye trusts us because we came here with you. You can't leave us alone with him; it's not fair on him or us. We need you Paul!'

'I'll be there, trust me,' he demanded as he pulled away. I pulled him back and dared to place an arm around his shoulder. He struggled to free himself and I felt the alcohol anger kick in. His body stiffened. I should have let him go free; he could have easily beaten the crap out of me. Instead I slipped my hand across his chest and squeezed him into a headlock.

'You can hardly walk, you mad bastard,' I whispered into his ear. 'You haven't got a hope of catching a horse. Come with us. Please bro?'

He looked deep into my eyes and then nodded. We started down the track after the others. Paul was limping badly and was obviously in some pain. I called a halt and asked to see his wounds. He grimaced, peeled off his shirt and pulled down his jeans. Despite the blackness of his skin the ugly bruising was easy to see, and several gashes required torn shirt dressings. He hobbled on, grumbling about how much easier it would be on a horse.

It was getting dark, and I had to will my exhausted body forward. I had been on the go now for well over ten hours and knew it would be another two hours before we regained the beach. The torches we had borrowed began to die as we reached the grasslands. We had just enough light to see the short black snakes that lay on the track, drinking the last of the sand's warmth. Whatever they were doing out at dusk they were still full of energy, and flicked angrily away when we disturbed them. Taipans. Very poisonous.

The torches gave out and Mick and Paul led us gingerly onwards through the darkness, their bare feet tentatively searching out each new step. At this rate it would be past midnight before we made the beachhead. Eventually Susie took charge, brushing aside the blacktracker egos as she forged to the lead in her hiking boots. No snake dared hang around as Susie stomped us to the ocean.

From the crest of the high dune we saw a big fire burning brightly on the beach. Above, flashing with neon-energy, hung the Milky Way. At the far end of the beach a fire threw a large circle of light around a group of people — our hosts and friends. We raced down the dune and across the sands, only to find that the stream was running deep with the tide. Stripping off, we carried our clothes on our heads and waded into the black water. The tide sucked at our bodies, seducing us towards the deep, as our tired feet searched for traction amid sharp and slippery rocks. I struggled, exhausted, up the final slope to the firelight circle. The air was warm and still and the sand soft as a doona as I collapsed onto it. We were fed oysters for supper and the two Popeyes told us Dreamtime stories. The tales encompassed the epic sweep of the stars above our heads and the formation of the beach on which we lay. Age-old stories explained the awesome beauty glimmering in the starlight. Murri girls again swam across the sky and watched as a snake cut valleys into the mountains.

As the camp settled down for the night I carefully worked an opportunity to be alone with Popeye PK.

'Popeye, I want to talk about tomorrow.'

He looked at me and nodded.

'We are aware that the cave is a men's place. The women know that, and realise that perhaps they shouldn't see it. I don't want you to think that because we are white visitors that the laws should be relaxed.'

He quietly laughed at me. 'Perhaps no one goes. We'll see.'

When I finally lay exhausted beside the fire I had the widest smile on my face. The last twenty-four hours had been surreal for the suburban boy. Kidnapping an old man, calming a knife fight, wading though taipan snakes, speeding through ocean waves, wrestling a drunken friend, eating fresh oysters and being lullabied beside a fire with ancient creation stories. The coals warmed me, the stars mesmerised and the sullen slap of slow surf on sand sent me to sleep.

I awoke with Popeye's foot in my ribs.

'Come on boy, wake up. You want to go to the cave, or what? Old Popeye and me, we bin dreaming. Everybody goes to the cave. Come on, get those girls moving, get those boys up.'

Oysters for breakfast, and a billy on the fire for tea. PK told us that both he and the other Popeye had received the same dreaming during the night. We were all welcome to visit the cave. We were anxious to be off on our great adventure, but Popeye made us wait until he'd had a second mug of tea, and a third. Finally he gave the signal and we raced up the beach and climbed the rocky, wooded slope that rose above the north end of the bay. We stood outside the mouth of the cave as Popeye slowly climbed towards us.

'You need not have waited,' he wheezed as he reached us. 'You could have gone in.' But I could tell he was glad that we hadn't.

It was darker inside and, as our eyes adjusted, we stood in reverent silence.

The cave was about the size of a small bus and absolutely covered in paintings and drawings. This was no museum; it was a living gallery, with fresh works supplanting images of the ages. Particularly important paintings were carefully retouched by the elders, Popeye explained. The others blurred into an abstract mural, paintings upon paintings that seemed to date back thousands of years. Among the more traditional depictions of animals and other beings were unusual images — geometric designs, a sailing ship, strange symbols.

'You fellas can talk if you want,' offered Popeye, but I sensed he was glad that we hadn't. But then we did, pointing out things of interest and discussing oddities. Popeye also spoke and told stories about visiting the cave as a child. He was relaxed. Eventually he turned to leave the cave and we all started to follow.

'No, stay longer if you wish,' he said, and left us, trusted us, on our own. Gradually my companions left in twos and threes. When the final couple were ready to leave I chose to stay on my own. As they left the cave I heard a sound. The moment I was alone I heard it. I almost called them back, but an instinct told me not to. I stayed and listened ... to breathing.

I couldn't imagine what animal could breathe in such a rhythm. Very long breaths, with drawn out silences between in-breath and out, and out-breath and in. Very deep, low ... but unmistakably real.

All I could think of was carpet snake. Nothing else but a large python could breathe so slowly, could it? I knew they were harmless, but this one must be huge. I tentatively searched the cave, heart beating nervously. No snake.

I stepped outside to search for a hidden ledge where a snake might be hiding. I found only solid granite rearing above the mouth. Outside, everything seemed normal, if a sweeping, gumtree-framed view of a deeply blue Pacific can ever be thought of as normal. It was peaceful and I could hear wind, not breathing.

I stepped back inside the cave and the breathing was louder.

Slowly in — silence — slowly out — silence — slowly in —

Impulsively, I did something very peculiar. I lay down

on the sandy floor and tried to match my breathing to the pattern I was hearing. I had never meditated at that time of my life but for some reason I went with the flow and joined in. It wasn't easy. The cycle was slow and I was panting. I was scared. Shit scared. There was no snake, no mammal, nothing — except breath. This was something weird.

Slowly in — silence — slowly out — silence — slowly in —

At first it was impossible. I was trying to force my panting breath to slow down instead of calming my racing heart. I greedily sucked in air too soon and my lungs hurt with the effort. I surfed a wave of panic or two. Eventually my slowing breath calmed me down and everything became easier.

Slowly in — silence — slowly out — silence — slowly in —

I became aware, totally aware, of my surroundings and myself. My senses were wide open. I listened to the breathing and heard my own breath singing the same song. I heard the waves on the beach, the wind in the trees, the blood pumping through my body. I could taste the oysters from breakfast and the salt from my swim, could smell the sea and my sweat and my dissipating fear. I felt grains of sand beneath my skin, a bead of sweat rolling down my neck, the breeze blowing across my body, the cool of the cave and the warmth outside. I saw the paintings on the roof above me in vivid detail and felt the light change as clouds and leaves moved outside.

I was aware of all this and more, yet I wasn't thinking. For the first in my life since I'd started talking I wasn't thinking. I wasn't even thinking 'Hey! I'm not thinking.'

There was just no thought for a long time.

No mind, no intellect. Just waves of awareness passing through me. Deep down into the ground beneath me, and out of the cave and around the bay, my awareness flew. I became the centre of the universe, and an insignificant point within it. I was a part of everything and more alive than I'd ever been before.

Slowly in — silence — slowly out — silence — slowly in —

Then there was a voice in my head. 'Okay Phil, you've been here long enough, piss off.' It was my own voice, but they weren't my words.

I leapt from the floor, out of the cave, down the slope and onto the beach without a backward glance. I saw Popeye in the distance, ran up and drew him aside. I babbled out my experience and waited for an explanation from the expert. He just looked at the ground and drew pictures with his toe.

'It might have been the spirit of the cave telling you, a whitefella, that it was right for you to be there,' Popeye finally concluded. 'Or it might have been that spirit saying it was wrong for you to go.'

He turned and left me to my own wild thoughts. I didn't want to be alone. I wanted to share what had happened and make sense of it all. I searched for Paul and found him lying in the healing pool, a brackish black pond of warm water, and told him my story of the cave. Like most blackfellas I have since told I think he was a little jealous. He desired such experiences for himself. Living in the city he needed confirmation in his soul that he was still a real Murri, that the ancestors and spirits could still reach him. Paul was particularly needy for such things, and it angered him a little that I had stayed and received what he regarded as a blessing. He should have been the last person in the cave.

'It's punishment for being drunk,' he angrily decided. 'I've lived too long in the city, I'm fucked. The magic'll never come to me.' With that he stood up and stepped out of the pond, water streaming from his languid limbs. There was no limp. His cuts had healed over without scabs. There was no sign of yesterday's injuries. I called him back and pointed out this evidence of magic. He stared in awe at his unmarked skin and marvelled as he flexed his muscles without a stab of pain.

'Magic,' he muttered, and grinned. He returned and we sat together up to our armpits in magical medicine water, feeling our limbs go soggy. Feeling blessed.

It seems strange now that I wasn't more in awe of the therapeutic qualities of the billabong. I had seen Paul's cuts and bruises virtually vanish before my eyes, and just accepted the impossible as matter of fact. For several weeks I was, however, full of wonder about the breathing cave. I couldn't shake it from my mind. What had happened? What did it mean? Why me?

In the meantime we toured around the vast district, performing our play for Aboriginal communities. We would arrive in a new location, meet some elders and more of Paul and Mick's relatives, and choose a flat central space to play on. We would build our stage and backdrop with the help of local kids. Just before show time we would tour the community, spruiking and gathering a flock of children. The adults followed their kids and when everyone was settled *The Murri and the Martian* began. The play was a comic book style sci-fi adventure involving an Aboriginal kid and an alien child who has run away from his flying saucer. It had songs, dances and jokes about colour (the alien was very green).

In Mareeba the show started so late it was getting dark,and we used the headlights of our hired mini-mokes to light the stage. For special moments we flashed into high-beam. At one community we dared to perform in front of the beer canteen, which got noisier and noisier and eventually ugly. Several rocks were hurled at the stage, but we battled on and finally won respect for our tenacity. We played to the Murris who live in the park in Townsville, and encountered on Palm Island an extraordinary mixture of hope and despair, paradise and hell, welcome and rejection.

In Mosman we discovered the falls, a series of rapids in a vigorous river which cuts deeply through limestone hills. The gorge there is sacred to the local people, but also a great tourist attraction. In those days, the early eighties, eccentric redneck conservatives governed Queensland. Well, they conserved what they thought worth preserving, principally their own privileged lifestyles. When the tourist operators complained about the eyesore that was Mosman Aboriginal Reserve the government response was to move everybody to the other side of town away from the gorge. Away from the sacred place so that middle-class tourists could drive to the white-water paradise without having to witness blackfella squalor. Away, out of sight, so that visitors could frolic amongst the rocks without their consciences being pricked.

Naturally the local Murris refused to go. The government, out of spite, built new houses for them in the wrong place and refused to put any money into the reserve. The old concrete houses fell to pieces. The eyesore degenerated further. Rubbish bins overflowed, flies carried disease from open drains, despair oozed from the houses and broken bottles littered the ground.

Some of the local kids helped us to clear a space and rig our set. As our makeshift theatre was emerging from the rubble I noticed a nervous tourist walk down the road from the gorge. He kept walking past the reserve, glancing anxiously at the community until he saw my white skin flashing in the sunlight and came over to me.

'Excuse me. My car's broken down. I've left my wife and kids back down the track. Do you know where I can find a mechanic?'

'No mate. I'm new here myself.'

'Is there a phone I can use?'

'Not that I know of. I'll ask these guys.'

I saw a sudden look of fear strike the man's eyes as I talked to the Murri mob. One of the kids ran off and came back with a tall young man.

'You got car troubles mate?' he asked the sweating tourist.

'Yes, down the track. Can I phone a mechanic from here?'

'We got no phones, but we can fix cars. I'll come with ya and have a look if ya like?'

The man's face was a story to behold. He was scared shitless of taking this big black man back down the track to his family, but also scared of what abuse he might get if he rejected the offer. He was scared of leaving his family alone, and scared of returning with a wild blackman.

'Go on,' I gently encouraged. 'Let him look at your car. He'll probably fix it.'

So the two of them walked back up the track. There was distance between them, the distance of ten thousand years and half the world. An overweight office worker and a skinny warrior.

Thirty minutes later the car pulled up and the young mechanic climbed out. There were smiles on everybody's faces and it was clear that the kids idolised their saviour. The wife thanked him with a huge smile and the men shook hands. The car drove off with a flock of cheery waves. By a simple act of offer and acceptance a huge gulf between races had been bridged.

But then I had trouble of my own. As show time approached our audience began to disappear. We discovered that they had all run into their broken houses to squat on the concrete to watch television. The program that had dragged them away from our play was none other than Doctor Who. The world was acting its absurdist best. Here we were about to perform a sci-fi play in an isolated Aboriginal community only to have our audience stolen by a BBC drama about a space/time machine. We waited for the good doctor to finish his adventure and then ran around the community knocking on doors and dragging people out to see our show.

I foolishly ran in bare feet. As I was running towards a group of women I felt a strange sting/slap sensation in my left foot. When it next hit the ground it seemed to fold in on itself. There was no pain, but it felt like all the tension had gone from my flesh, as if a balloon had burst without noise. I looked back and saw half a broken beer bottle with its jagged peaks capped with blood oozing slowly down the glass. I propped myself on one foot, lifted the other and turned the sole towards my face. My flesh was deeply ripped. The skin flapped. My foot felt dead. Blood dripped to the ground.

The pain came later, as a bush doctor opened the wound to check for glass and then threaded the sides of my foot together. There were nights of throbbing pain and regular excursions into agony as I cleaned the gash to ward off tropical infections. Within a week we were back on Popeye's land. Under my foot was a zigzag scar I will carry for life. Despite the difficulty of hopping through the bush on one foot I carried the wound with a strange sort of pride. I had an absurd sense that it was fitting. This trip, with all its adventures and insights, had changed me, opened me. I chose to see the scar as confirmation of a deep transition, and promised myself that every time it itched I would remember.

On our last morning, whilst the others packed up the camp, I sat on the mission beach and watched young boys with wild eyes racing horses bareback. Popeye appeared from nowhere and strode towards me. Since our return from the cave he had returned to a dissolute life, had bent again into an old man. This morning his back was as straight and his eyes were as clear as they had been at his beach.

'You were the boy in the cave?' he asked, knowing the answer. 'I bin thinking about that. Thinking a lot. I bin think it was the spirit of the cave, the beach, telling you, a gubba, a whitefella, that the spirits still live. They not some nonsense made up in the head of the blackfella. They live. They breathe.'

Popeye stopped talking to look at me. To look into me. He studied me for a while and I imagined I could feel him probing me somehow. He exhaled slowly, nodding to himself, and spoke again.

'And I think "Why?" Why did the spirits speak to you? Why you? Why a whitefella? I think it is because you tell stories. You are the boss of these people who come here to tell us stories of your world. Now I think you have a new story to tell your own people. Go home now son. Tell your people that the spirits still live.'

And so I was given a quest by an old Aboriginal magic man. I had to find a means by which to tell my fellows that the spirits live. It is a difficult, almost impossible, quest for a white Australian. We are a nation with a healthy cynicism not given to flights of fancy. We have few remaining taboos, but talking about spirituality is one of them.

At first, to honour Popeye and the magic breath, I made a couple of weird works of theatre and dance. I was desperately attempting to convey something so extraordinary that it inevitably passed right over the heads of the audience. They loved the shows but missed the point. Which wasn't surprising, as I had no real understanding of what I was saying about non-western cultures and their concepts of the sacred.

The longer I lived in the city the harder it became to hold belief in the breathing cave. Without the stars and the tropical breezes and knowing black faces the memory became a phantom. I rationalised the experience as a youthful folly, as a result of strong exertions, little sleep and too much sun. I lost the sense of its magic, forgot the power of the breath. I allowed Popeye's interpretation to become the kindly ramblings of an old man. I resigned from the quest.

Necklace

Before Popeye gave me his message to deliver I was already caught up in other streams of weird waters. I seemed to attract these things. Why? What made me so different? I think the first thing was being born a twin. From the moment of conception, or a split second afterwards, I was marked as different. My single cell of being was instantly lonely and split to form another entity. And then there were two. Or maybe there were two spirits wanting the one body. Whatever, I entered the world as an identical twin brother, forever linked with another human being.

It is hard to gauge the effect of twinning. In those pre-fertility drug days we were rare and often the centre of attention. This can either build or destroy a person. Thankfully we flourished. Having a mate continually alongside saved us both from the worst ravages of peer pressure. I remember one of our first 'grown up' high school parties. A bunch of younger girls of the rougher variety had been enticed along, and beer was being guzzled by the gallon. Down by the back fence clothes and decorum were discarded and drunken young female bodies were welcoming all comers. Our close friends were in a quandary, whether to prove their manhood or obey their qualms of conscience. John and I had no such problem. We discussed the situation rationally, agreed that we both felt embarrassed and simply walked home. Our friends later confessed that they solved the dilemma by getting so drunk that they collapsed without having to take action.

Twinning did not, however, keep us clean and virtuous forever. As we grew older and life began to offer all sorts of dangerous opportunities our partnership gave us the courage to step off the stage of conventional behaviour into the orchestra pit of depravity and politics. Of all our high school's graduates it was John and I who ran fastest towards new experiences. We protested Vietnam and apartheid, sat-in university offices, tried drugs and street theatre and hung around the most interesting people we could find. Emboldened by each other we ran away from suburbia as fast as we could.

Being a twin was a bitch when it came to relationships. I wanted to scream whenever a girl said 'I don't know which one I like the best' and then avoided going with either of us. Eventually we had enough of each other. I went to Europe, he went east. We didn't see each other for three years. This allowed an interesting test of our deep connection. One night in Sydney John awoke from a frightening nightmare in which he saw me on a yacht, battered by huge waves and eventually washed away. As he knew that I was sailing across the Mediterranean he was deeply troubled and desperate for me to contact him. When at last I did we discovered the amazing fact that at the very moment that he dreamed I was being smashed around in a storm I was actually in the middle of a dead calm. That pretty well sums up the amount of psychic power shared by the two of us. Our genes may be identical, and much of our behaviour, but our spiritual lines must have disconnected at birth.

My first adventure was going to university. It was only across town from the new suburb where we lived, but it was like another universe. Those were the days of the Vietnam War, when the campus was alive with fiery debate and political rage and a belief that we could make a difference. I sat in on strange lectures with brilliant teachers, learnt to lay out a newspaper and run a rock and roll gig. I soon got bored with party politics and manifestos and discovered drugs, sex and theatre.

I hate to admit it, but it was fun to be at war. We were forced to battle with the forces of convention, with the government, the police and our parents. This freed us in a way that these days acknowledging gayness seems to do. Having rejected the old world we could paint our own whatever colours we wished. We wore outrageous clothes (or none at all), grew long hair, danced in the streets and yelled our beliefs through megaphones. We believed we could change the world, and in a way we did. That was good for our self-confidence. This quiet suburban kid found his voice and enjoyed having pride in his convictions.

Of course our brutal youthful righteousness was bound to come a cropper eventually. My fall from grace came in small and relatively painless increments as I saw more and more of the real world. I never hit conventional reality too hard. There were many lessons. For instance I had despised my fellow youths who agreed to go to Vietnam until I met a veteran, and his story broke my heart. The guilt for all the abuse I had thrown at the poor bastards ate away at me for some time. I think that was my first inkling that I did not know everything, that my generation could actually be wrong. Not in our opposition to the war, but in our abuse of those who had gone because of their own immature moral convictions.

We were all immature, and it hurt to realise.

Lots of learning, lots of fun and a healthy sense of my own fallibility. University gave me a lot of gifts, but there was nothing within those prestigious portals that led me to seek spiritual knowledge. I had studied science and medicine and gained a sense of the scientific method. I was a bad student, but I was a believer. I knew that science could explain all, or would one day. I had no time for God. I believed that we humans had developed past the need for superstition. I was still a believer in scientific orthodoxy when I dropped my studies and found a career in the theatre. Things began to change only when Launi and his necklace entered my life.

I first met my wantok in the courtyard of my drama school in Melbourne. First day back at school in second year and there stood this exotic stranger in the middle of the quadrangle. A mass of tightly curled hair and beard, a short stocky body wrapped in a new green jacket, and skin the colour of tropical floodwaters. A warrior from Papua New Guinea (PNG). I was instantly drawn to him and a friendship quickly grew between us. Launi was fresh from the Highlands, a young actor in the big city for the first time. I diverted him from the city crush and techno-madness with walks through the botanical gardens ('Are the black swans good eating?'), and with weekends at a friend's little cottage in the hills. He slept on the floor in front of a log fire and filled my mind with images of his homeland.

I had no inkling of the importance Launi was to have on my life. Later I would discover that we are strange doppelgangers, white and black, and our lives are bound together. Back then we were just friends. And he gave me a necklace.

It was a circle of snake vertebrae, interspersed by a number of pig tusks and one dog tooth. It was bleached with age into a yellowed whiteness, hard and brittle, strung on a length of handmade string.

'This is my father's necklace. He gave it to me. Now I give it to you, Phil, my wantok.'

'It's extraordinary. I'm honoured. Are you sure? Is it meant to be separated from your family?'

'You are of my family. That is the meaning of wantok. You are my brother and so you are my Poppa's son. He gave this necklace to one son, now it moves on to another. And one day you will bring it home to Niugini. It will make sure of that.'

And so I became the custodian of an ancient artefact. It lay beside my bed and every night I marvelled at it before drifting off to sleep.

Launi had come to Australia to train in western theatre methods. He was already a wonderful comic and mime with a strong and expressive body. The plan was for him to return to his company, the famous Raun Raun Theatre, and eventually, perhaps, direct it. There were doubters in PNG who feared he would become culturally corrupted in Australia to the detriment of his traditional work; however neither Launi nor his company founder believed this. The Victorian College of the Arts had arranged a very flexible course that allowed him to move freely through all the different opportunities available there. He could avoid western specialisation and concentrate on those skills that would be of value in PNG.

In a bar one afternoon he urged me to go home with him. He wanted to demonstrate to the doubters that the skills he was learning in Melbourne would be useful at home and that his outlook had not been corrupted. He decided that the best thing was to take me home with a show the two of us had created that would prove the accessibility of his new training to Highland audiences.

I wrote to the twenty-five largest companies in Australia begging for dollars for this 'important cultural exchange project,' and we started to rehearse two plays to take. The content and style of the work was a difficult decision. Should it be dance based, to cut across language barriers, or abstract, or mime? A serious work to demonstrate the power of drama, or a celebration of two cultures working together? The problem was solved when we went to see the Marx Brothers in *A Night at the Opera*. At the point when Harpo sucked his boss's toupee up a vacuum cleaner my wantok screamed with laughter, jumped from his seat and repeated the gag over and over to me as the film moved on. The audience members behind us eventually moved angrily to the front, but I was very happy. The Marx Bothers style of slapstick was obviously a universal theatre form. We decided to work with physical comedy to tell a relevant story.

Launi explained that urbanisation was perhaps the biggest problem facing contemporary PNG at that time, and so we created a sort of Dick Whittington pantomime for two. *Radio Play* told the story of a young village man seduced to the big town by the promise of easy money. Instead he experiences poverty, theft, cultural breakdown and greedy businessmen. We also created *Stick Fight*, a slapstick acrobatic argument between an Australian and a Niuginian. We wrote and rehearsed and Launi flew off to PNG to prepare the way. I was to follow.

But the time came and I had no money and no passport. I had my ticket, but there was nothing left to live on. And I had foolishly told the PNG consulate that I was not a tourist but an artist working with Raun Raun Theatre in an unpaid capacity. They didn't know what to do with me, so sent the passport to Port Moresby, where it disappeared. And then I lost the necklace.

I had been living with a group of fellow actors in the inner city, and just before I was to follow Launi we shifted house to a beautiful crumbling mansion in a bayside suburb. Unpacking in the new house I discovered that the necklace was missing. I felt awful that I hadn't realised this earlier, that in the frantic party/house-moving/going-overseas-any-day-now excitement I'd failed to keep track of my keepsake. Everything in my new room was unpacked at once in a frantic attempt to find it. We returned to the old house for a final cleaning, but it wasn't there. I was very upset, and went outside to cut down the knee-high grass in the back yard, my mood better suited to ploughing aggressively through the weeds than cleaning the toilet.

I suddenly stopped the mowing. I don't know why, but in the middle of a long stretch of overgrown lawn I just stopped, de-throttled the motor and walked around to the inlet to the rotor blades, bent down and picked up the bones. At that moment I hadn't been thinking of the necklace, I hadn't consciously sensed it. I wasn't aware of why I stopped or why I walked around and bent down. I just did it. It was only later when I pondered on these simple actions that I realised I had no control over them.

At the time I was just thankful that I had saved the necklace from a ghastly destruction. I carefully examined it for damage. I guessed the dog had taken it out there, or perhaps a rude or confused guest at our final party. Whatever, it wasn't damaged in the slightest. I knew it so well. Except that I didn't remember the dog's tooth, which seemed to have changed. But that was too weird to contemplate, so I dropped that line of thinking and just hugged the necklace to my chest.

'I'm sorry, I'm sorry,' I muttered. 'I'm sorry. I'll never do that to you again.' Then Whack!!! A searing blow to my forehead. Stars and blackness. The whole cliché. I awoke seconds later (I assume), flat on my back with the necklace lying on the centre of my chest. It looked smug. Above me stretched the clothes hoist. I'd walked smack into one of its arms. It looked smug too. And I felt as if I'd been given a warning. 'Look after me, I can kick.'

Back at the new house the mail had arrived. Four envelopes had cheques from big businesses, one made out to double what I'd asked for. In another envelope was my passport. I was on my way. There was one detail left to take care of. Launi had mysteriously ordered me not to take the necklace back to PNG. Not this time. Not on any account was I to bring it home. One day, but not yet.

So what was I to do with it while I was gone? The encounter with the clothes hoist warned me to treat it seriously. After much careful thought I left it with one of my new housemates. Joe was a lecturer at the drama school, the oldest and most responsible member of the household. He had works of art himself and knew how to treasure and look after special objects. He was happy to oblige, and placed it high on a shelf in his room.

So when I was first in Papua New Guinea, the necklace stayed in Melbourne. I returned two and a half months later exhausted and elated. On my first night home, amongst all the celebration and traveller's tales, Joe led me aside. He took me upstairs and pulled a carefully wrapped bundle from behind a hidden cupboard door.

'I couldn't live with it in my room, so I hid it here safely until you returned,' he explained. He had awoken one night to voices. Wondering who was up so late he'd gone out into the corridor to find the entire house wrapped in dark silence. Back in his room he could still hear distant conversation. Again he checked outside, but nothing was stirring. Slowly, he came to realise, with a growing dread, that the voices came from the necklace. As he moved closer he could hear them, deep within, but also a long way away. He carefully wrapped up the bones and placed them safely at the other end of the house. He hadn't heard anything since.

I took the package into my room and unwrapped it tenderly. A circle of snake vertebrae, pig tusks and one dog tooth, bleached with age, hard and brittle, strung on a length of handmade string. I lay it carefully beside my bed and contemplated Joe's story. Strangely I wasn't worried. Whatever the magic the bones possessed I was sure it meant no harm to me. In fact I felt protected.

I breathed in its mystery. It smelt of Papua New Guinea. My mind was full of the last few months. Niugini!

Niugini

I knew that Niugini would be utterly different from anywhere else I had ever been. I had had only one brief experience of the tropics, on my way home from Europe, but that was sufficient to awaken my excitement.

Having missed connecting flights, my companion and I arrived in Kuala Lumpur as the airport was closing down for the night. A small fleet of expensive taxi drivers were eyeing us off. The tourist counter was closed but an officer there was working late and offered us a lift into the city. I assumed he was simply an office worker, but we left the airport in a chauffeured limousine, and he delivered us to a cheap, clean hostel and arranged our booking, at local prices, for the few nights we had to wait.

The next day he picked us up and took us to the jungle wrapped hills to visit the Monkey caves, flashing his laminated card at security to allow us to wander through the limestone caverns freely, without guide or fellow travellers. On the way to visit his family for lunch, Ismail brought us to a jungle clearing. This was his land, he explained, and he was considering building a simple lodge that could be rented by Western travellers to allow them a little experience of the rainforest.

As we spoke a group of traditional hunters walked

down the track towards us. I was struck dumb at the apparition, and even Ismail seemed amazed to see them. They, however, in their loincloths and painted faces, seemed completely at ease in this meeting with a white couple and a business-suited Malay. They chatted freely to Ismail, and soon I was trying out their blowpipes and examining their bows, marvelling at their make-up and smelling their hair.

Ismail gave me two special gifts. His benevolent treatment of me (a ragged, long-haired traveller) completely contrasted with the prejudiced view of Asian bureaucracy I had constructed from the horror stories of acquaintances. He was also a charitable Moslem, which did not align with tales I had heard of the Islamic disdain of the infidel. In other words, he destroyed a few deep preconceptions and taught me to use my own judgement when in contact with other races. He also gave me a momentary taste of the exotic nature of traditional lifestyles. Those five minutes with blowpipes and painted faces carved an indelible impression.

I was remembering the smell of that jungle, and picturing large leaves and dangling earlobes, as I lay on a train bunk travelling through Queensland on my way to PNG. I had decided to travel by rail and fly from Cairns so that I would have time to rest and acclimatise to the tropics, and prepare myself for the unexpected.

Of course nothing does prepare you. Not for the smells and bustle and variety of tribes at Port Moresby airport. Or the flight up PNG's central mountain massif and down into the fertile wonder of the Goroka valley.

A whole new family met me at the airport. New sisters and fathers and mothers and cousins and babies who are uncles and an old man who is my nephew. I struggled to remember names and relationships and take in all the sights. We seemed to be surrounded by mountain ridges, and hundreds of Niuginians in colourful clothes and weird hats swarmed outside the airport fence.

We camped at Launi's father's house which was at the back of the airfield, a corrugated three-bedroom dwelling on low stilts perched on the edge of community gardens. There were ten adults in the house and countless kids. Meal times were quite peculiar: the food itself was a strange mix of local garden and tinned supplies, but it was the eating which was really weird. Everybody was using their knives and forks in completely different fashions. Some squeezed the implements between odd fingers, others twisted their wrists. My new Poppa twisted sideways and bent his body backwards over his plate to get his fork into his cau cau (sweet potato).

A few days later, after eating with some fellow actors, I realised what was going on at home. When we next ate I pretended I had trouble with my knife. I threw it and the fork down onto the floor on which we sat and reached for the food with my fingers. Everybody's cutlery tumbled down in unison. The family sighed and grinned, and laughing with relief reached out and took handfuls of steaming greens and sweet potato.

It was Momma who had demanded the family buy knives and forks for me, to make me comfortable at meal times, and insisted everybody use them. It was a lovely gesture. Momma was a very small, very thin woman who hid from me most of the time. She served me food, and watched me, but kept her distance. She spoke no English and we communicated with smiles. Most of the time.

Every week or so the family held get-together evenings when all the relatives sat in a big circle and one by one performed items to entertain. Some would sing, some dance, some tell jokes or stories. They were lovely affairs, and I determined to have my fire-eating gear ready when the next one occurred. It was the spectacular success I expected it to be. Children screamed in fear when I ate the flames and let them play on my skin. Simple tricks really, but good fakery magic. The family cheered enthusiastically as I went inside to put the sticks and fuel away.

Momma launched herself at me. This tiny woman who had never said a word spat a tirade in my direction. The words were foreign, but the meaning was clear — 'What on earth were you doing playing with fire. You stupid boy. The children will copy you and get burnt. Fire is dangerous. Do that again and you will burn.'

I never ate fire again. Not in PNG, and not back home in Australia. So vehement was her response that I feared she had some sense of an impending accident. To be able to eat fire one needs control and confidence with the flames. Momma shook my confidence from me and I gave up the silly business.

Poppa Doiki was small like his wife, but his thinness was formed from knotted gristle. He had been a strong and vigorous man, but was now old and worn down to bone and leather. He had walked PNG with the Australian kiaps (the bush patrol), opening new land and introducing isolated cultures to Australian law. He originated from coastal Papua, but had elected to stay in Goroka near to the white explorer he had served with distinction. He had led an exciting and unusual life and was still very active.

Some of the young men I began to hang around with told me that Poppa Doiki was a magic man. It was reputed that he could travel across the mountains in spirit form. He was well liked but people were wary of him. Launi wouldn't tell me much and Poppa himself seemed like a gentle soul to me. I couldn't see the shaman in him, but one night I tasted his power.

Launi was involved with some business with an uncle from the village on his mother's side. This was the rich uncle, the first in the village to make use of the new systems and get a loan to buy a coffee plantation. He had become a big man, a rich man, and wanted Launi to join him. Launi spoke excellent English; he studied in Australia, and was thus of value to him in his business.

One night Launi got very drunk. He had been behaving deviously for a few days and had behaved badly in the hotel. He demanded I give him a lift to his mother's village and to prevent him from further public embarrassment I agreed. He said he wanted me to come with him because his uncle had a gift for him and I had to be there for some reason, but when I asked more questions he just became demanding. I refused to drive all the way into the village without more information and we began to shout at one another. Finally I dropped him off in the rain on the track to the village and, as he tramped away through the mud, he continued to abuse me.

Hours later he turned up at Poppa's house with a car. He was so drunk he had driven it into a ditch and was yelling for me to come to the village with him.

'You come with me brother,' he bellowed. 'You come with me or you are no longer my brother. Come now, or you are no longer my wantok.'

I ran from the house to quieten him down. He wanted me to see his new car. He wanted me to drive it and him back to the village. He wanted me to see him accept his car from his uncle. I didn't know what he was talking about and, feeling strangely apprehensive, refused to do his bidding. He got very aggressive and was shouting at me in pidgin when his father's voice cut across his noise. Poppa made a sharp whistle-like sound and Launi shut up at once. Poppa looked at him, glanced at me and then swung back to his son with a glare. He then nodded at the house and back to his silent, quivering boy.

'Go and sleep under the house with the dogs,' he ordered quietly.

Launi slunk away and the red sports car remained in the ditch. Yes, red sports car. That was the gift, the bribe. Launi told me later that if I had returned with him to the village it would have meant that he had formally accepted the car from his uncle. From that point he would have been his uncle's man. He would become a businessman and would no longer have been a man of culture and tradition. It was a major crisis moment in his life. I felt uncomfortable that my influence was so important even though I had no idea what was going on. I was discovering the secret power of the white man. We have far more influence than we deserve and we must be careful.

The prevailing wisdom of whitefella travel in PNG is to remain careful at all times, preferably by remaining safely in town behind hotel security. Bugger that. I was there for adventure and insight, so despite torrential rain and difficult roads I jumped at any chance to get out of town and into the 'real' Niugini.

One night I was a special guest at an all night singsing. Saio, Raun Raun's resident clown, had invited me to visit his village an hour and a half's drive from Goroka. Hundreds of people from three or four villages had gathered at the singsing site, a bamboo circle of verandahs facing inwards. A huge fire burnt in the centre. The dancers wore tall bamboo contraptions lashed to their hips and backs. These rose twenty feet into the air and were covered in spring-loaded, multi-coloured feathers that flicked in time with the music on every step. It was a simple shuffle dance around and around the fire that went on for hours and hours. The beat never wavered, the pulse was insistent as the trance of the dance was established.

Around midnight I was taken aside by several men who attached one of the feathered contraptions to my back. It was surprisingly heavy for a costume made to be worn all night. They led me into the dancing circle. I had assumed that the dancers were pushing themselves into some form of ecstatic state, but if so, my arrival completely destroyed that. I created much merriment with my attempts to get my feathers bouncing in time with the music and, for half an hour, the sacred became the silly.

Later I fell asleep beside the fire, to wake several times before dawn as whirling bodies continued to dance around me. The beat hardly changed as the night progressed but the dancers thinned and fell to the ground. The survivors swayed onwards, faces slack, eyes unfocused. It seemed as if their conscious spirits had left their painful bodies, which danced like zombies around the flames. I wondered where their souls had gone and what they were experiencing during the agonising ecstasy of this all night shuffle.

Meanwhile, we rehearsed our play in Goroka and added several actors to our troupe. We played a number of performances opposite the thriving markets on the football oval, where hundreds of people packed around us and lapped up the show. It was a big success. Launi could breathe easier seeing that his new skills were appreciated by his people. And they loved me. I don't think they had ever seen a whitefella act the clown before. Certainly they had never seen one so prepared to make fun of his own culture, or to throw himself around so acrobatically. I became a minor celebrity in town and was rarely left alone. Strangers would sidle up to me on the street and begin talking and holding my hand. As the performance was in pidgin English it was presumed I spoke the lingo, so I spent many hours listening to a torrent of words I barely comprehended. Eventually my ears became accustomed to the rapid flow of words and I began to understand.

After a few weeks we headed out of town on tour. First we drove west, up and through the clouds into the badlands of Chimbu and down into the fertile valley of Mount Hagen. Then back east and down the magnificent Markham valley to Lae. From Lae we flew in a small plane out to Umboi, the largest of the Siassi Islands.

The Siassis were one of the cultural homes of Raun Raun Theatre. The company, whilst based in the Highlands, consisted of performers from all over PNG. The minute island of Aramot in the Siassis was represented by a disproportionate number of actors. The music and dance of Aramot was particularly vivid, and Raun Raun had arranged for us to take our show there as an exchange for all the young people the community had lent to the company.

As we waited on the beach near the airfield for the boat to Aramot an old man spoke to me. My pidgin had improved and in the style of old people he repeated the words of his story until I understood. He pointed to an island out to sea and told me that was where Jesus had stood when he arrived at Siassi. Wherever his feet landed islands had grown. He had cut the estuary, on the shore of which we sat, from the living rock with his axe. Jesus? I was appalled. I assumed that missionaries had usurped the creation myths of the locals and replaced the name of the local god with that of Christ. This made me very angry, but as the old man continued to talk I realised that there might be another interpretation. I interrupted him and had Launi translate my question.

'This man who came and made the island and the mountains. I call him Jesus. What name do you give him?'

'Kilibob.'

Ah. The missionaries hadn't corrupted the story. The old man had used the name Jesus to help me comprehend. He knew that I wouldn't know Kilibob, so he used a word for a deity that I could understand. He was sharing his story with me in the only way he could. The names of the gods were interchangeable; it was the story that mattered.

Aramot is a small, sandy atoll a kilometre or so off Umboi. It is about the size and shape of an Aussie Rules football ground, with every inch of beach covered in outrigger dugout canoes. There are a dozen coconut trees grabbing a little space between the cramped huts and a central community square. At one end of the island is the men's house and at the other the women's, each with a toilet and club and ritual space.

Always there is activity. When the moon rises canoes venture out to the reefs. Before the sun sets the fishermen and gardeners return to the island. High and low tides offer their own rhythms to human activities, as do awe-inspiring electrical storms which bring the people out to the beaches to marvel at the heavens.

Touring shows to traditional communities is utterly different from the one-night-stand tours prevalent in Australian rural areas. It is bad form to just arrive and perform a show. There are elders to meet and the local calendar of events to respect. We were asked to wait a few days until most of the islanders returned home from trade and fishing trips.

Throughout New Guinea our comic morality tale about a young man tempted to the city had produced much laughter. As well as laughs we often received compliments from the elders for showing their young men the dangers of town and importance of home. In one village a long meeting of the men was held after the performance so the community could thrash out the play's meaning. Everywhere we had received enthusiastic applause.

But in Aramot they just stood silent. No laughter, no talking. A dead audience. We worked our bums off with acrobatics and slapstick, cunning jokes and naughty asides. Nothing, no giggles, no smirks. We couldn't even see any grins, for throughout most of the play the people had held their hands over their mouths. It was a horrible experience, playing comedy to an unresponsive audience, but we ploughed on.

Eventually we came to the scene where I appeared in a 'fat' suit, snorting like a pig and greedily rubbing my hands together. I am a conniving white businessman who scrambles in the dirt like a pig at the very thought of money. At that moment, towards the end of the play, they suddenly broke into laughter. The whole village exploded in mirth, their hands forced from their mouths with great sneezes of suppressed glee.

We found out later that the island chief, who had officially welcomed us before the show, had given instruction to his people. In the island language, which none of my fellow actors spoke, the chief had said: 'These people have come a long way to tell us a story. One of them is a whiteman, so it must be important. If anybody laughs there is going to be trouble!'

With the show performed we were able to simply relax and enjoy island life. I swam with the boys and speared fish from the reef. I chewed betel nut with old men and swapped jokes with the young ones. I befriended Peter, an actor from Port Moresby who had met an Aramot girl while dancing with Raun Raun Theatre. When she became pregnant they married and he chose to return with her to the island to await the childbirth. This is unusual behaviour for a Papuan man. Generally the women follow their husbands to a new village after marriage, or return home for the birth without their husband. Peter, however, was a city man with a passion for his country's culture. Although he had danced and sung to traditional music from all over the country he had never experienced village life. The marriage and pregnancy gave him that opportunity, and he found himself on Paradise Island. He was an invaluable source of information and organised little adventures for me.

I rode to the big island on an outrigger, perched above the hollowed logs on a woven platform, as barebreasted women forced their paddles through the tropical waters and sang songs from the sea. Giant fruit bats flapped silently through the jungle as we paddled upriver to the fresh water and fertile gardens. We returned to Aramot laden with food and water, leaving behind the mosquitoes and dank humidity of evening.

One morning, after catching and eating breakfast, I sat with several children on the beach. A young boy crawled onto my lap and examined my skin with great interest. He rubbed it and ran his fingers through the hair on my arms. He was particularly fascinated with my blemishes, my freckles and moles. He tried to scratch one away and lifted my arm to his eye to peer closer.

'Wat dis?' he asked.

'A mole.'

'Mole,' he repeated. 'Mole. Me savvy. Dis mole, em hole. Hole in your skin. Underneath you black like me.'

Like all small communities, however, there are periods when things can get a little dull. Then it is time for Tamberan Man.

As a special guest I was shown the sacred bilas (or costume) of Tamberan Man. There were four or five hanging from the roof of the men's house. The bilas consisted of pointed conical masks that perched upon a man's shoulders, reaching nine or ten feet into the air. Below them hang grass skirts that completely cover the wearer from the head to the feet, except for their protruding arms. Amid much excitement I was dressed up as Tamberan Man and allowed to parade around the men's compound where the community at large could not see me. The way I walked, with my white arms poking through the costume, provoked much laughter.

Then one of the initiated men dressed up and became Tamberan Man. At certain times of the year suitably qualified men could become Tamberan Man and walk out into the village proper. This, I was seriously informed, was a dangerous activity for the rest of the people, for any women or children seen by the spirit man would have to be killed. For them to even know who was inside the costume was punishable by death. As a special treat for me Tamberan Man then walked through the gateway and out into the community. I was aghast; I didn't want any deaths to occur for my entertainment. I tried to call him back but the spirit had taken over and the giant ignored my pleading.

The effect was dramatic. A call went up immediately and the entire island was galvanised into action. Women and children screamed with terror and ran into hiding. Black bodies sprinted across the sands, women called desperately for their children and people crushed into tiny spaces and covered their heads. A bunch of kids stretched out behind a coconut palm, moving in a disciplined line around the tree as Tamberan Man passed by, six children hidden by one thin trunk.

I saw a toddler playing innocently in the sand become scared by all the activity and start to cry. Tamberan Man began to turn ponderously towards the noise as a woman dashed courageously from behind a house, plucked the little one from the dirt and dived and rolled away beneath a verandah just as the huge eyes of the monster turned her way.

My horror turned to astonishment as I saw more fully what was going on. Once safe the women and children were silently chortling. The heroic mother was congratulated for her bravery and laughed with pride. Adolescent boys snuck up on Tamberan Man and deliberately made a noise to cause him to turn. But he turned so slowly that they had time to hide again.

It was a huge game. The screams and terror were pretend, the adrenalin palpable, but the penalty of death was not really an option. This Tamberan Man was never going to see anyone. It was an ecstatic, exhilarating thrill ride for everyone, which stirred up the village for the rest of the day.

Women whispered to me later that they knew who the man was because his rings were showing. They said it was impossible for a wife not to recognise her husband's feet but they must never let on to the men that they knew who was inside the costume.

Of course there are more serious sides to Tamberan Man. Should he ever speak (which is the preserve of only the most important of the elders) then he must be obeyed. I was told of a recent time when Tamberan Man had demanded that certain coconut palms on the mainland were to be left alone as they were being ravaged by the growing population and losing their value as a community cash crop. This order was obeyed. When the community wellbeing was threatened, or if major taboos were broken, the power of Tamberan Man was absolute. As I understood it, the men's council would debate such issues, and then send one of the elders out as the Masali to command the people. I was also told that the spirit of Tamberan Man had the power to affect his human counterpart; that there were spiritual matters in which the human merely became the beast of burden for the god/spirit who rode upon his shoulders.

I was assured that whatever use Tamberan Man made of his human carriers, and vice versa, the penalty for wrongdoing was always death. It was up to Tamberan Man whether he was enjoying a farce, or if it was for real. And that was part of the delicious game that was played out on this island paradise.

This gentle island community was new on the world scale of things. Some forty years ago a cyclone had ravaged the island. It had taken every tree, every hut and every person. After the disaster there was an immediate scramble on the mainland to take possession of the little spit of sand and coral. The families next in line moved over to Aramot. A twenty-minute paddle from the 'mainland', the island was relatively insect free. In the early morning the people commute inland to the rich soils and fresh water upstream beyond the mangroves. When the sun gets too hot they leave behind the bugs and stifling dankness of the jungle and sail home to cool sea breezes.

On the way home they stop at a sandbar that lies a hundred yards to the north of the island. It protects Aramot from the worst ravages of tides and currents, and from breaking waves which, though rare, can attack the island without warning. Dugouts returning from the mainland with fair winds will load up with mainland sand and dump it on their way home. Every child is expected to visit the sandbar every day to leave behind a handful of sand. Piccaninnies too small to walk paddle across in bowl size canoes to leave their offering. Every day a handful of sand for paradise. What the ocean takes the humans replace. Their home is protected so they may live there forever.

A handful of sand for paradise.

After Aramot we walked around the Umboi. Our show was a great hit in Kampalap and Aupwel, two vigorous coastal villages, although this was tough touring. It was constantly hot and humid and the paths between villages snaked up and down ridges and through swamps.

One night we stayed at a Catholic mission high school. The show went very well but the white priest did not trust our roving band of actors. He gave us an empty shed in which to sleep and then padlocked us in to keep his girls safe. Under the light of a kero lamp we observed our quarters with dread — a bare room with a concrete floor covered in ants. That night we developed a strange ritual to allow us to grab a few hours sleep. We poured kerosene in a circle around us and set fire to it, then killed every ant within the circle. Under the light of a second fiery circle we lay on our sarongs and closed our eyes, so exhausted from the day's walking and our performance that we quickly fell asleep. When we were wakened by the returning ants crawling over our bodies, we lit another circle and started again.

The next morning we were miraculously saved from a ten-hour walk by a boat that was heading up the coast to the next village. As we cruised north the jungles and mountains of Siassi steamed to our left, whilst to the right a blue-grey massive ridge of mountains appeared through the horizon haze. It was West New Britain. It didn't look like Britain at all. We trawled through leaping tuna and managed to hook and drag one up onto the deck. It made a worthy gift for our hosts when we jumped ashore.

After our show there was a six-to-six. Six-to-six is a pidgin term denoting a dance from dawn to dusk. Two ukulele bands played throughout the night. Each band consisted of one guitar, three ukuleles and a bamboo bass. The bass is made up of varying lengths of hollow bamboo, struck on the open ends with rubber thongs. Neither band knew more than six songs, but they happily rotated them throughout the hours of darkness. During the evening the men danced with each other on one side of the square, the women at the other. Towards midnight the white missionary arrived with clapping hands and a loud voice. He treated everyone like children and told them they must all be in bed by one o'clock. They cheerfully agreed and continued the segregated dancing. The Father returned an hour later and ordered them to go home. The dancers begged for one more dance, and the priest left.

Nobody retired and the man of God never returned. Once he had gone for good the sexes started to mingle on the dance floor and eventually in the surrounding bushes. Either the priest was very naive, or he was satisfied to have done his duty and leave his flock to their carnal desires.

The next day's walk was a rough one. The track wound around the coastline, and for miles ducked and weaved through a forest of mangroves. Pulling up boot after boot from sucking black mud was exhausting in the humidity. When we finally cleared the trees I spied surf breaking off the headland and, peeling off my sticky clothes, I swam out towards the waves. My companions yelled dire warnings about sharks and pukpuk (crocodiles), and the idiocy of white men, but I was luxuriating in the refreshing tranquillity and I ignored them.

The relief was short-lived, for within minutes of restarting our hike the sweat was pouring again, boots rubbed and the slogging rhythm of the track took over. How much longer now? Will we be at the next village soon? Voices from up the track encouraged us and soon we found people. They welcomed us with smiles and the news that their village was 'klos to nau'. What exquisite words of torture. Close to, now. For the next couple of hours we expected a village around every corner.

When we eventually staggered into Oropot we found a paradise, but over it hung a shade of darkness. The village was beautiful. It had a wide grass avenue dividing two lines of well-kept huts and a deep freshwater pool from which the ocean could be seen. Before we could relax, however, there was a hurried meeting of important men. They were happy to host us for as long as we wished to stay but, unfortunately, we would not be permitted to perform our plays. They understood that we brought laughter and, due to a recent calamity, laughter was taboo. I caught up with the full story once we were floating in the pool, legs and feet joyful at the release from boots and gravity.

Two nights prior a young woman had been mysteriously killed and the entire village was in mourning and alarm. To have a murderer within their midst was an awful occurrence for such a small and tight-knit community. I was amazed at their readiness to accommodate us with such generosity at a time of tension and sorrow, but we were constantly assured that the problems had nothing to do with us, and that we were honoured guests. I chose to lie back and enjoy the hospitality and fresh spring water.

That night I was wakened by the sounds of chanting. I crawled out of the pitch-black hut and struggled to see what was happening. There was just enough light to see Launi sitting on the edge of the verandah staring out into the gloom. As my eyes adjusted I saw that he was tense and sweating. I crawled quietly across to him. 'What's happening?' I whispered.

'Ssssh,' he replied, 'I can't tell you'.

I sat and listened to the chanting. The kundu drums were as a heartbeat, the voices both rough and melodic, powerful yet pleading. I strained to see something, but the night was moonless. After some time my need to know got the better of me.

'What's happening?' I whispered again.

'Ssssh, I can't tell you.'

'You can tell me,' I pleaded. Launi looked at me, and realised that I wasn't going to shut up or go to bed and decided I could be trusted.

'All right,' he whispered. 'They are having a ceremony to find out who killed the girl. They have a piece of bamboo they use to call a spirit to discover the killer. Now be quiet!'

This information shocked me. Now I understood the significance of what I was hearing. With the girl's unsolved death haunting the community they had called upon sorcery to find the truth. I leaned back against a bamboo support and listened and waited. A strange energy seemed to gradually build up, but whether it was within me or emanating from the darkness I was unable to tell. The hairs on my arms and head started to stand out from my body. The air was charged and I was frightened.

Suddenly a dull red flickering light appeared. It seemed to be amongst the voices and had an immediate effect on the chanting, which slid up a key and increased in tempo. Then the light brightened and began to glide up through the village. It seemed to me that the voices were following the crimson glow, although I could still see nothing of the men, for strangely the light did not illuminate its surroundings, or throw shadows. It was dullish at that distance, but the impression was powerful.

As suddenly as it had arrived the light vanished, but the chant continued at its new tempo until the light burst forth again. This time it was much brighter and was welcomed with charged voices, the chant now higher pitched with increased tempo and very loud with excitement. For a moment things held still, the voices as if in praise. Then the light shot away, towards us for a terrifying second, and then it was zapping around all over the village. It appeared to be skimming at grass height and was quite brilliant, but still it failed to illuminate the ground it covered. It shot around the open spaces as if searching for something, like a manic electric bloodhound on the trail of a scent. I shrunk back into the hut in fear of the power of whatever it was. Then, having traversed the entire village in only a few seconds, the light lifted off the ground and shot into the sky. It must have burnt even brighter as it flew, for it was plain to see as it shot out of the valley and high into the sky, up and up as it climbed over the adjacent mountain ridge and away. It was truly astounding, powerful and impossible.

I sat in a slump, trying to make sense of what I had seen and what it could mean. I heard the men follow the light out of the village. Launi and I said nothing. I was mystified. How could such a bright light not shed light? How could any object race so close to the ground with such precision and control and then have the power to fly mountains? I had no doubt I had witnessed magic and that the light was some sort of entity that moved of its own volition. Such thoughts were almost as terrifying as the event itself. My understanding of the world was suddenly very shaky.

I was brought back to reality with the return of the men. They sauntered towards us with kerosene lamps, smiling and relaxed. Some joined us for a cup of tea. No one mentioned the ceremony or its outcome, but it was clear that the great tension we had felt in the village had been lifted. Someone said something and everybody laughed. The laughter taboo was broken. I learned later that the 'masali' (spirit) had indicated that the killer was not from the village. Thus community trust was intact, and laughter was again allowed.

It took us another week to return to our base island of Aramot. We crossed the central ridge of the main island and walked down to the sea. There we slept for three nights in a stinking copra store (it took me a long time to eat coconut again) and then piled aboard a coastal ferry. It was the start of the school year, and older children were returning to their studies at the central mission and on the mainland of PNG.

I climbed onto the roof with some of the young men to

escape the diesel motor below which belched acrid fumes all over the passengers. As we motored up the dramatic coastline we stopped at every village along the way. At each stop we were greeted by outrigger canoes loaded with enough bags of food and supplies to last their children for a term of schooling. The canoes then returned to shore to pick up the passengers, and more and more kids climbed aboard. By the time we reached Aramot (the last stop before the mission) the boat was dangerously overloaded with hundreds of children and it wallowed in the swell like a pregnant hippopotamus. I was very glad to be ferried ashore.

My friend Peter raced up to me as soon as we had landed. He dragged me away from Launi and the other actors. 'I need to talk with you,' he confided as he pulled me to a relatively quiet corner. 'I need your perspective, some weird stuff happened while you were gone.'

I sat on an old house stump and waited as Peter, normally eloquent, struggled to know where to start his story. It was a problem I recognised and have experienced subsequently. How do you tell a whitefella about stuff that white men are not supposed to believe in? He sized me up for the third time and plunged in.

'Just after you left a girl died, a healthy young woman. Everyone was very upset. Then two nights ago they held a ceremony to find out who killed her. The men gathered under those coconut palms over there, and began to chant and play kundu. I hung around and joined in, it's not hard to pick up a chant even if you don't know the language well. So we sang and danced for hours. The same chant over and over. I went through boredom, and exhaustion, but eventually there was nothing but the chant and the beat of the kundu and the stamping of my feet. And then, suddenly, this piece of bamboo —'

The deja vu resolved itself. I realised with a jerk that Peter was describing an event parallel to the one I had witnessed in Oropot.

'Suddenly this piece of bamboo, which we had been dancing around, lifted off the ground. By itself. Like magic. Just lifted up and flew, glided, over into that house. That house there Phil. If you had been here, you would have seen. I am an educated man, Phil, both of my parents teach at the university. All my life they have told me that magic and sorcery are primitive nonsense. I believed that, until two nights ago.

'When the bamboo came out of the house there was — there was — this — this spirit, a little man, this — I don't know what! It sat on the bamboo like it was riding it, but sitting sideways. It had a big head, with big eyes, and big mouth. It looked around, and then it looked at me. Right into me, and then it laughed at me, and spun the bamboo round and shot off across the ocean.

'Everybody's happier now. The old men say the killer is not from here. He's from over there, over the sea. They say he's dead now, when the spirit man gets him.'

We sat quietly for a few minutes and then I began to tell him what I had seen in Oropot. We compared experiences and sat dumbfounded by the evidence. We considered mass hallucinations as an explanation but couldn't believe they accounted for what we had witnessed. The uncanny similarities of our experiences on either end of the Siassi Islands ruled out, in our minds at least, any possibility that we individually somehow imagined or dreamed them. Although he had seen a spirit man and I a flashing red ball of light, we had no doubt that we had experienced similar events. Perhaps the vigour of his chant and dance had allowed him to see things more clearly than Launi and I, who had merely wakened from deep sleeps.

We sat talking for hours. The villagers and my travelling companions left us alone to our deliberations. A plate of fish and rice was carried over, and mugs of hot sweet tea, but nobody bothered us. Even the kids, who day and night had clung to me like flies, kept their distance. The sun dipped and disappeared and still we talked. The sky flared with colour and turned black, storm clouds built and flashed with lightning but we just looked at one another's faces. Two scientific, western educated men, one black and one white, realising they had witnessed evidence of a world with spirit entities that could search and laugh and see right through you. Peter asked me if I had believed in a spirit world before these strange events occurred. No, I hadn't.

I told him about a time at university when a few of my friends began to dabble with a ouija board and reported some bizarre results. I had laughed at them. There were no such things as spirits and ghosts, I confidently declared. They challenged me to participate but I refused until they called me a coward unwilling to put my scientific dogma to the test. If you want to get an Aussie to do something, you challenge his courage. I went to the next session.

I arrived at a friend's dining room to find an odd assortment of folk. One was Rob, a self-styled anarchist who was also there to take the piss. We were both stunned when the glass moved so smoothly, spelling out words. We both confessed to trying to stop the thing, but it truly seemed to have a volition of its own. It spelled out the name of a certain old church to the north of the city. Still laughing, half-scared, we drove out. As we approached the church a bolt of lightning flashed from the sky and struck a solitary tree in the middle of a field. It burst into flames as we passed.

As if that wasn't enough, the church was pure Stephen King, surrounded by the graves of pioneers and poplar trees. A slight mist was gathering. We hung around the car park pretending it was fun. Rob demonstrated his revolutionary materialism by breaking into the church, and called us all over. The moon shone through the stained glass windows, and I was relieved to find it strangely peaceful. We started to relax when suddenly we felt, rather than heard, a deep thump from beneath the floor. It scared the shit out of us, until we began to rationalise causes. It must have been a truck on the highway hitting a bump, or explosives in a quarry in the hills. Another bump, perfectly silent. At that we fled the scene.

I had no idea what to make of it all and chose to ignore it. I left the group and dedicated myself to theatre. Others couldn't let it go. I heard of more seances spelling out names that were later discovered on headstones in the cemetery, and of near death experiences with black cats and trenches dug in the road. I stayed well clear, my scepticism strong and theories rational. The most ghastly thing I saw was Rob — the former anarchist and social revolutionary stealing Hieronymus Bosch and other religious art books from the university library — becoming so caught up in it that he dropped his political radicalism and became a haunted loner studying medieval symbolism. He lost his spark, and that scared me even more than the bumps in the church. I swore then never to dabble in magic and reconfirmed my belief that it didn't exist.

Peter had relatives who believed in ghosts (as do the vast majority of the people in PNG) and they would tell stories of strange happenings, but manifestations had never occurred in his presence. The world had seemed to him completely rational until yesterday. His sense of the universe changed the moment the bamboo lifted from the ground before his eyes.

I told him my father's ghost story, of when he was a kid in a big old house in Scotland. The old woman who lived upstairs had died and the old dogs she had left behind had pined for her. The dogs had sickened and my grandfather had them put down and buried in the garden. That evening, my father swears, as the entire family sat around the dinner table, they heard the door above them open and the old woman call her dogs, just as she had always done. And just as they always had, they heard the creak of wood and flurry of paws as two dogs raced up the staircase and into the room above. The door closed and all was silent.

So my family had experiences of ghosts just as Peter's family had. However, the rational sciences of the twentieth century had so influenced our lives that we no longer believed. Universities, it seemed, had demanded scientific proof of the spirit world and finding none had discarded it as nonsense. Peter's parents stopped believing. I stopped believing. The western world stopped believing. And here we were believing again.

As an electric storm strobed within gathering clouds, Peter and I explored this potential for another world. We continued to swap stories. He had been shielded in Port Moresby from the magic of the tribes of PNG, and the stories he had heard had always seemed ridiculous to him until now. I began to tell Peter about some experiences that I had while travelling for eighteen months through Europe in the mid-seventies. It was a fairly normal Aussie odyssey to the old country and continent. I hitched to the Arctic Circle and saw the midnight sun, visited the graves of great, great, great, great grandfather Rob Roy McGregor, marvelled at ancient cathedrals, galleries and glaciers, cycled around Cornwall, skied in Germany and sailed the Mediterranean. I listened to my Grandma Thomson's tales of the war and slogged through a dreadful London winter, earning enough to see a lot of shows, only some of which were brilliant. I got tear gassed in Paris and caught in the May Day riots in Barcelona.

I was learning the thrill and adventure of travel. I discovered that all my senses opened wide when I entered a new place. That when freed from the repetitive habits of home I saw and tasted and felt with a vivid gusto.

I wasn't in search of the mystical, but when in Rome, or London, one does as the natives do. Around that time I was fascinated by the concept of ley lines, the theory that sacred points of power throughout England and Europe (often indicated by ancient ruins, or stone circles, or chalk horses or churches) could be connected on maps by straight lines. I'm not sure why this attracted my attention. I think it was because it gave my scientifically trained mind a way of looking at ancient mysteries. These were the days of Von Daniken books on flying saucer men building the pyramids, and I was both enthralled by antiquity and puzzled by the gullibility of modern people. The ley line theory seemed to give me a chance to test things for myself.

I found myself walking on hillsides, lining up chalk horses and cathedral spires and old wells. They were lovely places to walk, but I found no shattering proof that some sort of energy field lay beneath the grassy ones, that the earth had its own acupuncture sites. Some places felt peaceful and others disturbing, but I gave it little thought.

Then one day my friend Janet and I hitchhiked to Glastonbury Tor, a lone hillock that rises from a depressed plain in the south of England. It had become the focal point for neo-Druids and ancient hippies, and our driver turned out to be an acolyte. He told us that on midsummer night the energy of the universe was conducted through the tor to make fertile the soils of merry England. The more he prattled on the less I believed. As he dropped us off at the bottom of the hill he insisted that on our way down we should visit the medieval well on the other side. 'The spring water,' he assured us, 'will blow your minds. It's better than dope.'

It was a glorious English day with those animal shaped clouds which fluff across the sky. One of those days they invented the word 'halcyon' for. It was a steep little hillock a few hundred feet high, but we seemed to fly up its slopes. It was only once we were at the top that we realised that despite our heavy rucksacks we had run up like athletes. Neither of us was puffing in the slightest. This was before the days when I got myself fit, and Janet was not a runner. It seemed incredible. It was incredible. I stood against the age-old stone tower and let my mind swoop across the fields of England. I felt strangely empowered. I allowed myself to begin to believe that perhaps the paranormal did exist.

With a joy in our hearts we raced down the other side to the well. The promised crystal water beckoned as a champagne toast for the feast of the senses we had just enjoyed. We charged up a narrow lane (this time huffing and puffing, the magic didn't work on the way down) towards a wooden gate. There was a small sign hanging from it. 'CLOSED ON TUESDAYS.'

We laughed for hours. Even magic is run by public servants. Somehow the joke on us became the more significant experience; it is the one I told most often, only using the exertion-free run up the tor to build up expectations and set the scene for the gag. It is a typically Australian response to an experience of grandeur. Cut to the self-effacing joke and avoid talk of the supernatural. We are all for free speech, as long as you don't get weird on us. Quite understandable, but not very useful if you want to explore the profound.

I was telling Peter of my necklace and how it had saved its own life in front of the lawn mower. I mentioned that Poppa Doiki was reputed to be a shaman. The solid, safe world we had relied upon became distorted. New possibilities became apparent. In a world in which sorcery and magic actually worked, fairies and leprechauns were possible again. If by chanting and drumming men could call beings of power from another place and implore them to work for revenge, what other forces could be harnessed?

Lightning flashed across the horizon, green and orange, and we talked until we were both utterly confused — and changed. The certainties of science became chimera. My trained mind snapped a few sprockets and I began to accept things I had long rejected and reject the accepted. It was easy on that beach, breathing the balmy electric air of paradise, to spin away from my foundations. I am sure that it was that loosening that allowed me, a couple of years later, to hear the breathing in Popeye's cave.

Soon it was time to return to Australia. Before we left Goroka, I sat with Poppa Doiki and Launi on the back step of the house. After the island experience with red lights and flying bamboo I was anxious to discuss the spirit world with my poppa. Launi also wished to engage his father on such matters and, on that cool Highland night, he encouraged his father to talk. Poppa Doiki was unwilling. Launi wanted to know about his own powers, that had, apparently, been taken from him as a child. His father refused. Launi persisted. Did he once have powers like his father? Should he too have the ability to visit family and loved ones across great distance by spirit-travel? I had no real belief in such things as astral travel, but was fascinated by the dialogue and the significance of having a father who was a shaman. I asked too many questions and Poppa fixed me with his glare.

'Why you ask all these things?' he demanded, as Launi translated. 'You are too young to be interested in the spirit world. You are still just a warrior. In my world that is just the first stage of manhood. Next you will be a family man and then a community man who works for his people. If you are strong and hard working you may reach the fourth stage, that of the big man, a leader. Finally you will retire from the concerns of village life, from the concerns of others. You will be wise and have time on your hands. That is the time to embrace the world of the spirits and prepare for what comes next.'

Poppa could have stopped there; I was happy with that. But Launi kept badgering him about how he might regain his powers, and in frustration with his father's equivocation demanded to know whether I might obtain powers like the ones he sought. Poppa nodded yes. It was no big deal. Anyone could have them.

'Even me?' I asked.

'But think carefully my son,' he commanded me. 'Think carefully, do you really want them?'

'Of course I do,' was my first response.

'Perhaps not,' my second.

I thought deeply. I assumed that obtaining such miraculous powers would entail a quest and apprentice-ship of mythical proportions. I might need to live in New Guinea and study arcane rites and rituals, undergo initiation and trials and years of study. I might need to sacrifice my art and work and my love life and family and friends and all the comforts and stimulations of my western world. I realised that I did not have the drive, I did not really want the powers. I couldn't make the sacrifice.

'I don't think I'll bother,' I told Poppa, and he grinned with delight.

'I'll be visiting Launi in Australia during the year,' he told me as I stood to go to bed.

'That's wonderful,' I told him. 'If you need anywhere to stay we have a spare room.'

Launi, sitting on an empty flour drum, fell over backwards with laughter. From the ground he translated my offer to Poppa, who also burst into laughter. When he sobered he asked his son to tell me something and then leaned forward to study my reaction.

'Poppa won't be coming in person,' Launi informed me. 'When he comes he will come in spirit form.'

'Oh—' was all I could reply. I probably had my mouth open as I sat there in silence. Poppa looked at me with amused anticipation. I struggled to formulate a response. 'Um — tell Poppa he's still welcome,' I finally offered. Launi smiled and translated. The old man nodded and went off to bed.

These were the things I thought about as, on my first night back in Australia, I lay on my bed in Melbourne and looked at my necklace. It all seemed pretty wacky. I decided to keep the weird stuff to myself and only share the adventure stories. I thought about Poppa's five stages of manhood and decided I would wait for old age to explain the mysteries of the spirit world. I decided that I had no urge to go seeking arcane knowledge or chase gurus, not yet anyway. Instead, I realised, I desired to live a long and useful life. I was glad that I was still a warrior, yet looked forward to the next stages. Rather than repelling me, old age now held a fascination, for then I might discover the truth behind the red flickering light. But not now.

I wrapped up the necklace and settled back down into city living. I worked hard at drama school, fell in love and enjoyed life. Memories of magic diminished and sat in dusty diaries on my shelf. The world was solid again. I stopped believing in fairies.

Scream

Having made the decision to leave PNG behind — there had been a job offer with a theatre company as well as the possibility of training in the weird arts — I committed myself fully to my final-year studies at the Victorian College of the Arts. I discovered a lot of things about humanity and self. My body was forced into fitness, my emotions challenged and driven through hoops. In classes we played many of the games beloved by therapists, not in order to heal ourselves, but to free and know ourselves. A healthy reason to play them.

I learned to sing and I learned to dance. These are two of humanity's great joys, and entry to the spirit, but I had never tasted them fully. I was a suburban kid and had never trusted myself to really let go. You can only fully sing when you stop listening to your voice and just fly with the words and music. Dancing is even more primal and self-consciousness must be banished for the body to soar through space with rhythm and abandon.

I learned to trust my instincts and impulses (more suburban no-nos) and to shut down my intellect and rational thought in order to be fully centred in a performance. This for me was the hardest task of all. All my life my brain had been my advantage. I was clever and I had used it. Now I was required to let go of rational thought and judgement in order to let new experiences transform me. This was not an anti-intellectualism. On the contrary, we spent much time analysing, debating and researching. To build a character a lot of thought is necessary, but on the floor, in rehearsal and performance, it is time to trust in the hard work and just live in the moment. Just be. The same is true of the important, transformative moments in life. This is particularly hard for cynics to manage.

Hardest of all for me was voice training. We are not encouraged in Australia to like the sound of own voices, to speak up in class or society. Our culture teaches us to pull our heads in and not stand out in a crowd. I didn't like or trust my voice and knew that as an actor it was my weakness. It was loud enough, for sure, but had little subtlety, variety or vibrant power. I became secretly ashamed and hid my weakness by pulling back in class. I thus found voice classes boring and interminable.

On return from PNG I had a breakthrough. We had a gutsy American guest teacher, Rowena Baylos. She took no bullshit and her classes were fiery and manic. She drove me from my fears (which she saw through at the very beginning) and challenged me to become more courageous. We were working on Shakespearean soliloquies and in her very last class with us I stood before my peers in a run-down classroom and began 'To be, or not to be —'

I had done all the homework, the thinking and research and translations of archaic words. But now it all came together, and my mind stopped. The classroom and colleagues disappeared and the words vanished from my brain. I was arguing purely internally for an understanding of life and death. I was pleading for escape from my despair. My feelings were palpable. I was Hamlet.

I jerked out of my reverie with the applause. My classmates were beaming, they all understood my breakthrough and I was ecstatic for days. It was no miracle, my voice is still my weak spot, and I couldn't make up for three years of hiding in one morning. But the experience of otherworldliness, of transformation and powerful mindlessness was crucial to my future work, and my life. And conversely, perhaps it was such powerful experiences that allowed me to forget about Niugini. For a while.

One morning I was sweating hard in a movement class in a studio right in the centre of Melbourne, thousands of kilometres — and thousands of years — away from village sorcery. Bill Zappa, our teacher, had set up a truly weird, but inspiring exercise. After an energetic and thorough warm-up he asked us to study the bright red of the doors. He then instructed us to find an image provoked by the red and improvise a dance around it. Strangely melodic yet discordant sounds filled the room as we struggled to find images and start moving.

My first thought was of a fire engine. I danced a brief fire engine dance, feeling a bit silly. I returned to the door and saw a postbox. Try imagining a grown man doing a postbox dance. It was very static and banal. I beat a quick retreat to the door again.

Third time lucky. Now I saw red poppies in my mind, thousands of red poppies stretching over the landscape, each representing a young man killed in the mud of Europe. Now I was truly dancing. I smashed the floor in anger, spun in confusion and death, stretched my limbs and fingers in pleading and loneliness. I became wives and parents and children 'back home', and danced with grief and fear and loss. I became myself again, and let my anger at war and disgust at humanity fly out through my body and fill the room. It was a rare and powerful experience for me in that I was truly dancing without thought or judgement. I was the emotions, I was the horror. Eventually I was empty and came to rest, but not for long.

When you're hot you're hot and I wanted to keep on going. I raced back to the door for more inspiration. I wanted to keep dancing with this newfound ability to fly with my feelings.

Almost at once I was seeing the red flickering light of Oropot. I turned to dance a 'New Guinea spirit dance', but suddenly felt very apprehensive. It did not seem like a good idea to play with sorcery, so I let the thought drop and returned to the door. Only I couldn't make the image of a red flickering light leave my mind. I tried to concentrate on other thoughts, tried to form other images, but the light kept flickering before me.

Then it started to move. At this point it gets hard to explain. Somehow, I lost the sense of being in a dance studio in central Melbourne and all I could see was the light. It moved slowly, from one side to the other, and of its own volition. I began to feel fear as I sensed it watching me, stalking me. It slowly zigzagged towards me, and then picked up speed and rushed me. I ran backwards across the studio, miraculously avoiding my fellow dancers, and slammed into the dance bar on the wall as the red light accelerated towards me.

I bounced off the bar and onto the floor as I was enveloped in red. I curled into a tight ball and screamed in terror. I have never been that terrified, never screamed in abject fear, before or since. I let go of everything and screamed.

The red light vanished. I lay panting, shocked and empty, as one of my friends creatively picked up my scream and used it in whatever dance he was involved in. It sounded awful.

'Shut up,' I yelled, 'for fuck's sake, just shut up.'

He did. Bill realised that something dangerous had happened and changed the music into something relaxing and had us lay down on soft mats. He massaged my neck and asked if I was all right. I said I was and waved him away. I lay trembling, struggling to make sense of it all. The experience obviously had something to do with Papua New Guinea, so at the end of the class I asked Bill to arrange for me to miss the afternoon's rehearsal and set off on a couple of trams to find my wantok.

As I turned into Launi's street I had to climb over a stack of broken bricks which had fallen onto the pavement. I was still disorientated, and very relieved to find my brother home.

'Come in, come in, I am very pleased to see you Phil,' Launi enthused as he led me down a dark, cold corridor typical of cheap Melbourne accommodation. 'Sit, sit down. It is good you came, because I am stuck here and can't tell the college why I cannot go in. You must tell them what has happened. Two days ago I had a message from sister Eileen. There has been big trouble at home. Our enemies have been attacking the village with sorcery. Three people have died. At home when that happens everybody stays together indoors to build up community strength to beat the magic. I thought there was nothing I could do, being thousands of miles from home in a modern city, so next morning I walked out of this house to go to college. As I turned the corner a taxi shot out of the traffic and came straight at me. I jumped the brick wall just before the car smashed into it, right where I had been standing. So I ran home and stayed indoors and thought of the village. I am safe here. Will you tell them I won't be in tomorrow and why I have been away?'

'Happy to. I can't wait to see their faces. I bet they've never had that excuse before: "Unable to attend class due to sorcery attack." They'll love that one. But Wantok, the reason I've come is to ask your advice over something very strange which happened to me this morning.'

I told the whole story to my brother, about the red doors and fire engine and post box dances, of the passionate anti-war dance and red flickering light I couldn't control, and the terror which made me scream. He listened seriously, but when I had finished he was very easy and relaxed.

'This red light,' he nonchalantly asked, 'did it have a thin yellow line around the outside?'

Part of my mind said yes, but the other half was unsure. There was something about a yellow edge to the light that rang a bell, but my rational side decided I was probably making it up out of wishful thinking, or wanting to find an answer.

'I'm not sure,' I finally answered. 'It may have had, but by the time it was big enough to see properly I was in a panic and running away.'

'That's a pity. If it had a yellow line I would have known for sure that it was Poppa.' I was finding Launi's matter-of-factness about what I had described most surprising.

'I thought Poppa came to visit me this morning, in this room,' Launi explained. 'I felt him arrive and sit there, in that corner. I didn't see him, or his light — that is hard to do when you have been sitting around all morning. I talked to him as anyone talks to their father when he arrives at their house. I said hello, and I told him I was safe and staying indoors, and how I had escaped from the taxi. I told him I wasn't happy in Melbourne this year, that I was having arguments with my wife, that I wanted to come home, but that I would finish the year and he was not to worry. I sent my love to Momma and the rest of the family. And then I felt him leave. I think he came to visit you, then. He told you he would come and see you one day, you remember?'

I nodded. I had forgotten but now I remembered clearly. I saw Poppa back in Goroka sitting on the back step, with his twinkling eyes and ancient skin. I recalled inviting him to stay at my place and Launi falling back laughing. And I remembered telling him that he was still welcome if he came without his body.

'So after he left me I think Poppa came over to see you,' Launi continued. 'Imagine what he would have seen. What would the old man have made of all you crazy white people dancing to weird music and pretending to be fire engines? He would have watched that for quite a while. And you were dancing up a storm, thinking of your war, working hard, letting your feelings fly. When we want to see the spirits we dance and chant for hours, you remember what it was like in Oropot. So today you were in the right mood, or whatever the word is, to see the other-side when Poppa came to visit. So you saw his light.' Launi was laughing now.

'Imagine it from Poppa's side. He's watching this long-long (crazy) dancing when he sees you seeing him. What is this? White people cannot see the spirits. So he moves from side to side to test you, and your eyes follow him. Wonderful. His white son can see him. He is delighted. He throws out his arms and runs forward for a hug. "Son," he is yelling, but you cannot hear. You are so scared by the movement you panic and run away as he runs towards you. You scream and he realises his mistake, so he goes home. That is what I think happened. If you had seen his yellow line I would have known for sure.'

I slumped. I was baffled, disturbed, scared and worried that I might have offended my father by screaming in his face. The earth wasn't solid any more. I was free-falling again, and I didn't like it. Launi brought me back.

'Anyway Phil, some lessons. Red spirits like those are not to be feared, they are friendly. If any spirit ever bothers you, you should stand up to it, tell it to go away. It has no power over you unless you give it power. As you don't play with sorcery, and don't use its power, it has no power over you. Tell it to piss off if you don't like it. You understand?'

I nodded. I didn't know that I understood anything any more, but I understood his simple advice.

'And finally Phil, whatever you do, never, ever scream. Whatever it is, if it wants you and you scream, it's got you. When you scream you give up all power. Never scream. Stay strong, wantok, even if you are scared shitless. You savvy?'

'Me savvy wantok. Me long-long masta, tasol.' I burbled in my bad pidgin. I understand you Brother. I am just a stupid white man. I know nothing of these things. I was ashamed of my behaviour, of being a coward, of offending Poppa. But Launi didn't let me dwell on such feelings. He was excited that I had seen Poppa's light, and by what that meant about me, contemporary dance and the spirit of white men in general. He did not let me feel shame for long.

I pondered on these extraordinary events for a long time. Launi's simple acceptance of my bizarre experience, and his matter of fact interpretation that it was all Poppa's doing, led me to believe his explanation. I have tried to find other explanations but, apart from the possibility of a totally uncharacteristic psychotic episode, I can find none. I don't believe I went mad during that dance class, and it would be an extraordinary coincidence for me to hallucinate New Guinea spirit matters at the very time my PNG family was undergoing attack by sorcery. The two happenings must have been linked. Or so it seemed then, and still does.

I don't think that the Siassi lights and Poppa's light were manifestations of the same thing. The Siassi experience was of something other than human, thought it had been evoked by human effort. A malevolent sprite set forth through a bamboo gateway to wreak a little havoc and revenge before returning to whatever world it normally resides in. Poppa's light was human; it was he, or an aspect of himself, which somehow he was able to project across the world to find both a real and an adopted son in the big city of Melbourne. Both, however, indicate vast areas of knowledge, awareness and reality which contemporary science and technology have banished into the realm of make believe.

It was all too much for me. I hung onto Poppa's five stages of manhood and Launi's advice that if you didn't dabble with magic it couldn't harm you. I didn't dabble. I put it all aside. Except, of course, for that visit to Queensland and the encounter with the breathing cave, but that too soon shrank away into the mists of my mind.

I entered the second stage of manhood. My lover Lynn became my partner and then my wife. We struggled to build careers in the theatre and then struggled to have kids. The horror of miscarriage and wonder of birth replaced the adventures of warrior life. The trials and triumphs and tiredness of raising a young family dominated my time outside of work.

Our first baby, Ren, lived his early years in Albury-Wodonga where I directed a community theatre company. The company researched and told local stories and was very popular. We then moved to Western Australia where I created similar work and Nina was born. I became recognised as a very good director with Deckchair Theatre which became a great success. Without realising it I had entered into the third stage of manhood. I was a community man, servicing the vast village of Fremantle.

I lost track of Launi for many years. He had never been much of a letter writer but gradually all communication dried up. We grew completely apart but I sensed that we would meet again. I still had the necklace and he had promised me that one day I would bring it home. In the meantime it stayed by my bedside and travelled with me whenever I left home. It was good for me, a good luck charm I liked having around. My life was charmed, in that Lynn and I succeeded in having the children we longed for. I was happy, busy and tired. Life was very full.

Nearly a decade after losing touch with Launi I had the urge to create a one-man play. *Wantok* was a biographical work about my travels in PNG and Aboriginal Australia. A comic travelogue, a spiritual adventure through paradise. My opening night in Perth was terrifying. The actor's normal selfdoubts were magnified when mixed with those of the playwright, who was also me. It seemed ridiculous that anyone else would be interested in my life and I worried about the ethics of telling some of the stories. It was my first one-man show and it ran for ninety minutes and I was anxious about remembering lines and sustaining energy. I feared ridicule from critics and scorn from colleagues. To make matters worse I had no fellow actors with whom to chill out. My warm-up was clumsy and speedy. I was all over the place. I tried dancing and tripped, and my voice wouldn't come down from high-pitched nervousness. When Alan the production manager asked if I would clear the stage so he could let the audience in I begged for another five minutes, and reached for the necklace.

I had decided to use the string of bones on stage to help me focus in special moments of the performance. It was especially useful in evoking my memory of Launi when I needed to 'become' him in the show. Feeling the pre-show panic rise, I carelessly clutched at the necklace for comfort and it burst apart in my hands. The string broke, and snake vertebras and pig-tusks spilt onto the stage. I frantically tried to pick them up and sort them out and thread them back onto the stub of string. But my fingers wouldn't work, and I spilt the bones again.

'Can I let them in?' Alan asked.

'No!'

'Can I help?'

'No!'

I knew I couldn't perform the show with the necklace broken. It seemed sacrilegious, somehow. I sobered very quickly then and forced myself to calm. Alan held back the audience until I'd carefully ordered and slid each piece back into the right place, and tied an impossibly small knot with splinters of string. Such delicate work is not my strength. Neither is beatific calmness. But when I finally finished the repair, only minutes before the scariest opening night of my life, I felt strangely centred and peaceful. The show was a great success.

During the opening night party I went back on stage and thanked my skeletal serpent. And put it carefully away.

I had been desperately trying to find Launi during the lead up to this first season of *Wantok*. I had written many letters to PNG to try and find him but he hadn't been seen. A couple of years later I decided to remount *Wantok* for a fresh season and country tour. I had met a talented English director on his way to PNG and arranged for him to work with me for a week on his return from the exotic rainforests. He did some invaluable and inspirational work with me, but left long before the show opened. I sent a videotape of the subsequent performance to him in London.

I received a reply by return mail. On seeing the video both he and his partner were convinced they had met Launi in PNG. My portrayal of a New Guinean Highlander I hadn't seen for a decade was accurate enough for them to recognise him. Either I was a superb actor or the necklace had woven its magic.

Within a day I was talking on the phone to my long lost black brother. He had just returned to Goroka after years away. Apparently his training in Australia had spoilt him, so that he found it extraordinarily hard to fit back into PNG life. He had come back big-headed and began drinking. Eventually he had run away to dry out and restore his inner dignity. He found his peace hunting crocodile up the Sepik before returning to the modern world as a TV reporter and theatre director on the north coast. Now, just as I was ready to find him again, he was back home in the Highlands with a new wife and babies. I applied to the Australian Foreign Affairs Department for money to return to PNG to work with my bro on a new version of *Wantok*.

I completed my term with Deckchair Theatre and began to freelance again. Lynn and I raised funds to travel through the North-West with *Wantok*. We bought a four-wheel drive utility and trailer, and slowly cruised from Perth to Darwin. Mainly we camped rough and I performed in small communities, although occasionally we played the bigger towns. Camping with small children and setting up shows alone was tough work. Everything became reddened with dust and driving long roads began to lose its thrill. However the gift of performance that we offered gave us entry into unique communities.

We flew from Port Hedland into Punmu, a small community perched on the edge of the desert on the shore of a brilliant white salt lake. The people had been removed to the coast many years before, but had come back to their land to escape the grog and poverty of town. Here they could again practise their traditional lifestyle and walk their own territory. It was an eerie place with a constant wind blowing in from the low scrub desert. There was no way that I could ever live there, but the people seemed happy in their reclaimed place.

When I began to perform I realised that few of the audience understood English well. They were laughing and smiling, but not at my punch lines. I rapidly cut the show back, dropping the more verbally complex scenes, and improvised new comedy. I pretended to fall in love with an old woman, to everybody's amusement. The show hardly lasted half an hour and I felt a little sheepish about having flown so far for such a short show. However, that afternoon, when Lynn and I conducted a workshop with the local children, wonderful things began to happen. One boy who had apparently never talked in class began to join in. Several very shy girls also became involved. The teachers were thrilled by the changes and we talked about our success. I was sure that it had more to do with my morning's performance than with our abilities as teachers. Having seen the whitefella make a fool of himself the kids were prepared to do the same. Our normal whitefella façade of confidence and competence can have a debilitating effect on other cultures. When we allow them to see our weakness and foolishness we can become a little easier to handle.

Later in the trip, deep into the wonderful Kimberley, I had the privilege of sitting with an elder, Billy King, at my campsite. I had performed for his people the night before and I had invited him over for a cup of tea and chat. He told me stories about the early days of cattle stations and the modern difficulties of helicopter musters and lazy youths. Throughout our talk I noticed other campers walk past us and stare at the old fella. After Billy had left they came over to me echoing the same question: 'How do you get to talk to the Aborigines?'

Australia's tourism authorities have enticed travellers from around the world with images of Aboriginal people. There is a huge interest in the world's oldest living cultures and tourists hire vans and spread out across the north in an effort to taste the exotic. Of course the blackfella communities have not been consulted about the advertisements and few feel happy about being studied by overseas visitors. The communities have signs out the front telling strangers not to enter, and so the travellers hang about in frustration. Seeing that I had somehow managed to attract an Aborigine my fellow campers wished to know my secret.

It was my show that granted me entry, and a lot of hard work and persistence in faxing information and requesting permission to enter communities. It is not an easy thing and nor should it be. However, as I pointed out to several people, they themselves missed opportunities to make contact. Most days the local school had brought the children down to the waterhole beside which we camped and my family were the only ones to play freely with the kids. Another family, who were desperate to meet the locals, had a big yellow dinghy on the water which the Aboriginal kids had admired. 'If you had invited those children to play on your boat you might have made a lot of friends,' I pointed out. 'You would have had reason to talk to the parents and teacher, and who knows what might have developed.'

But the tourists were just as shy of the local blackfellas as the blackfellas were of the whitefellas. It takes a little daring to make contact, and patience to stay around long enough to allow relationships the chance to develop. People travelling too fast across the country, or being too precious about their property, will never meet the people. Politicians and government workers often make similar mistakes, expecting that by flying in and out of a community in an afternoon they can get to know what is happening. It doesn't work that way. In the Kimberley time takes longer to unravel than in other places. Only by investing time can the country and its people start to be met and understood.

In Kununurra I received the letter informing me of money and approval from Foreign Affairs to return to PNG. After performing in Darwin, we drove south and Lynn and the kids went to live on the coast of southern New South Wales whilst I flew north to the mountainous interior of PNG.

Launi told me not to take the necklace. I obeyed.

A Missionary Position

My second visit to PNG was spent mainly in the village of Massiafuluka, known as Massi to the locals. I lived there with Launi and his wife Pauline for six weeks as we rehearsed our new show and arranged a tour through the Highlands to Madang and then to Port Moresby. This Niugini experience was not woven with the same magic as the first. It was more domestic, in a Melanesian way.

Naturally, at the first opportunity I sat with Poppa who was living in Massi, Momma's village. He was a very old man now, with a massive mouth cancer and I had a great deal of trouble communicating with him. He remembered me, but had little energy for the rigours of translated conversation. I did ask him if he had visited me in Melbourne and he nodded yes, but when I tried talking about the dance class and the red light he withdrew. Launi told me that he had talked to Poppa as soon as he had returned to PNG and that his father had confirmed his spirit visit. I had to be satisfied with that.

On my second night in the village Launi and I had a few beers. It was our reunion drink and we became quite pissed as we swapped stories and caught up with each other's news. And as we did so, we started to become angry with each other. I had expected to find that Launi had become a big man by now. I had imagined him as a politician or head of a non-government organisation. Instead he was playing Gandhi by living in the smallest, most destitute hut in the village. He had thought that by then I would have become a big director of national importance. He was shocked and angry that I couldn't afford to fly Lynn and the kids in for a visit. Our voices became louder. We started to abuse each other. We were pulling each other down for the same reason at the tops of our voices.

After a while a young man came hurrying across the dried mud and spoke rapidly to Launi. He avoided my eyes. Launi dismissed him with an angry flick of his head.

'The elders just sent my nephew down to tell us to be quiet. They are shocked and shamed that I should yell at you in public. It seems you, Mr Whiteman, are a man of importance and that I have shamed my village.'

'Oh dear,' I giggled, and we fell into each other's arms with a burst of laughter that we suppressed by biting our fingers. White and black, yin and yang, but so much the same. It was good to be back with my doppelganger.

For the first few weeks in the village things were a little strained. Having a whitefella as a guest puts everybody on their best behaviour. This becomes a strain after a while. Husbands and wives cannot have arguments, children cannot be chastised and drunken revelry is banned. I felt the simmering tension building up but did not realise I was the cause. I don't think they did, either. Out of respect to one another we behaved so nicely all of the time that it became false. Normally Highlanders are emotionally spontaneous and honest. The pressure of suppression slowly built and we all needed an outlet.

It came in the form of a beating. I was in the hut when suddenly the peace was cut by the high-pitched screams of a woman, an angry male voice and the sickening thump and slap of a human beating.

'Stay in here,' Launi ordered and dashed outside.

The sounds of human pain and violence continued. Flesh hitting flesh, weeping and yelling. It was horrible. I sensed that if I went outside it would stop, but knew it was none of my business. I also knew that if it had been happening in my own country I would have tried to stop it, as I can't stand men physically abusing women. I think we all have a duty to stamp it out. But in someone else's village? In a different culture? I was paralysed with indecision.

Then another tirade, another ugly whack, another scream and whimper of pain. I couldn't help it. I went outside. My neighbour had a woman by the hair and was about to hit her again. Then he saw me and stopped. He dragged her into his house.

'You should have stayed indoors,' commented Launi. 'Now he will be shamed.'

'Perhaps he should be shamed,' I retorted. 'I know of no excuse for that behaviour.'

'The woman is his sister. When his parents died he took on responsibility for her but she ran from his influence and became a Two Kina Girl, a prostitute. He went to town and found her, forgave her and brought her home. He gave her his money so she would not be tempted again. But last night he was told that she still sells herself at the betel market. She admitted it and abused him for his concern. With AIDS and other STDs prevalent in Goroka he fears for her life. He was beating her to save her life and her reputation. Does that excuse his behaviour?'

'I guess so,' I shrugged. I realised that it was impossible to judge right and wrong in a culture radically different from your own. I didn't know if his actions were justified, but I did know I had no right to judge him.

When my neighbour showed his face an hour or so later I made a point of going to him and offering a cigarette. We talked for a while about the disco on the hill and other local concerns. We did not mention the beating or his sister. My chat with him was intended to demonstrate that I had not lost respect for him, to ensure he had not lost face. I think the word got around about the incident and my response. Almost at once people allowed themselves to be bad again. Nothing really nasty, just the occasional shout and swearing or argument. Somehow that also allowed a lot more laughter and joking as well. The village became accustomed to my presence and started to behave as normal. It was much more fun.

One evening we sat cross-legged on the floor of the woven bamboo hut Launi and Pauline called home. A low fire smudging the air, a broken kero lamp highlighting the smiles of my companions. It was Saturday night, and high above us on the hillside a Six-to-Six disco was raging. The village was showered with Afro-funk and Sepik-rock and 'C'mon baby, light my fire.'

The disco had been built on the ridge for the New Year festivities, a rough stockade of bamboo poles with a mud floor and big black plastic speakers. It was now late January but every weekend the gate take increased and the high-fidelity party boomed out across the valley. The elders were getting pissed off, but the young were drawn like randy moths to the bright light of good times and sweaty bodies the music promised.

'You going up the hill again tonight?' I asked Kopi, a handsome youth who, along with a number of his mates, had joined us for supper.

'Yes,' he grinned devilishly. 'Oh, there are many beautiful women up on that hill. We dance all night.'

'I think maybe there will be trouble tonight,' cautioned Launi. 'Many of the old people are angry at all this noise, and some of the fellows going up are very drunk already.'

'If they cause trouble the security will just throw them down the mountain,' Kopi argued. 'That is why so many women go, they feel safe. If anyone causes them trouble, over they go, down the hillside, over and over. It is very funny, and too steep to climb back up if they are drunk and want to keep fighting.'

'Will it go on until dawn, like last night?' I asked, fearing the worst.

'Of course,' grinned Kopi. 'Six-to-six, we all stagger down the slope when the sun comes up.'

'On a Sunday? Don't the churchmen get upset?' Massi village had seven churches in its small area. With such a robust display of Christianity I would have thought the Sabbath a little more sacred.

'We still go to church — we just don't go to sleep.'

'Until you get there,' laughed Launi. 'Sleeping, that's what church is for!'

'Launi!!' Pauline admonished sharply. She indicated my presence with a flick of her eyes, looked shamed and spoke pidgin English so fast I had no hope of catching a word. As usual Launi translated.

'She thinks I have offended you and wishes to know if you will be going to church with us in the morning.'

'No,' I answered Pauline. 'I haven't been to church in years.'

There was a sharp silence. Even the disco took a break as everyone pondered on the idea of a whitefella who has given up the church.

'But, but — the church is yours,' stammered Kopi. 'It —

white men — don't all Australians go to church?'

Kopi is a young village man who wants to know all the answers, who sees me as a key to the knowledge of the wider world. Constantly I am amazed at the picture these people have of Australia, all of us wealthy and happy, a land of bounteous paradise. And now, the conviction that we whitefellas are all churchgoing Christians.

'Most Australians do not go to church regularly these days,' I explained. Kopi and Pauline were shocked.

Launi laughed. 'When I went to Australia I thought I should go to church every Sunday,' he declared. 'Because in someone else's country you should do what they do. But then I found out that no one I knew was going, so I didn't bother.'

'No one?' stammered Kopi.

'You will burn in hell,' Pauline muttered. 'You could have gone by yourself.'

'Nobody I knew went,' replied Launi, answering them both.

'The churches are losing customers,' I explained. 'Except for Christmas and Easter, most of them are more than half-empty. As a nation we don't seem to believe any more.'

'So why do all the missionaries come here? Why not stay in Australia?' asked Kopi.

'Good question. I personally don't think they should be spreading an idea that most of their own countrymen question. That embarrasses me; they should try to win us back over first. But I don't think many missionaries are Australians anyway. You've got thousands of American missionaries here, and Germans and Dutch and god knows who else. Not to mention some very weird sects and fundamentalists you should be worrying about.'

'Why should we worry?' asked Pauline. 'They come to

tell the truth about Jesus. They educate and help us, set up aid posts and clinics. We are lucky they come.'

'It was the missionaries who brought peace to Highlands,' boomed a voice from the back. 'Before he came life was full of fear. All day you protect your boundaries and your women from enemy warriors. At night it is the sorcery you must keep away. The missionaries put an end to all that.'

'Some of them are good people,' I answered, starting to feel uncomfortable.

'But you don't believe in Jesus?' asked Kopi, eyes ablaze in the dull light. He senses a knowledge breakthrough. He wants me to give him reason to doubt his imposed faith, to allow him to break the rules that bind his young soul so that he can guiltlessly explore the mischief and evil he fancies.

Suddenly I felt the weight of the moment. Just as missionaries have won some of their power by the force of their strange whiteness and foreign knowledge, so have I the power to dissuade this young man from his church. It is mine to give him the freedom of his own morality, to set him adrift in Papua New Guinea's cultural confusion without a faith. I didn't feel equipped to exercise such influence.

'I believe in Jesus,' I finally tell him, trying to give up my life-altering power and keep hostess Pauline happy with me. 'It is the churches I have problems with.' (It seems I must still be honest.) 'Jesus spoke fine wisdom, his spirit was strong and true. But in the 2000 years since he walked on this earth hundreds of different churches have used his words for their own means and power. There are many good church people, but also many who destroy the cultures of other people, kill or steal their land in His name. I think these people are evil.'

'So how do we know which is which?' Kopi wanted still more answers.

'You know. Here you are very lucky. Around this village you have seven churches, even more in town. You have wonderful choice. If one preacher speaks the truth to you personally then that is the church for you. You have your ancient spirits in the mountains, and churches full of spirited singing and preaching. You can choose here. This country has great spirit, unlike mine.'

My arguments were confused, made up on the spot. Reggae rang down from the hillside, and I thought of Rasta and the evil Haile Selassie whose dope-smoking, sex-loving, dreadlocked, musical Christians had made him into a god. The fire smoked, Pauline tutted, Launi laughed and Kopi leaned forward for more white-man secrets.

I told them snippets of Christian history I had retained. Kopi was stunned by the news that Christ was not a white man and that the Bible was not written in English. I twisted through tales of Roman persecution, and of Constantine, the first Christian Roman Emperor who staged conferences to decide on dogma once and for all. (Yes, Mary was a virgin, as determined by a 60-40 vote.) I shocked them with stories of the inquisition and slaughter of the Aztecs, of sex crazed Popes, sectarian wars and Nazi Christians. I was also able to balance the tirade, with some uplifting examples of Christian martyrs, of great men and women who heeded Christ's simple philosophy and sacrificed their lives to improve the world.

The smoke and the music, the smell of bodies and the gentle snoring of sleeping children were all part of the magic of that night. A white man who never went to church turning preacher, trying to share a little truth and confusing everybody, just like all missionaries do.

Kopi clicked his tongue. The audience looked bemused. I laughed. Everybody laughed.

'Don't listen to me,' I pleaded, knowing that they were. 'I only know stories of what was, what has been. I know a little of a dying church, but not of a living church. You people have that. The spirit here is strong. I look ahead and what do I see? In two hundred years maybe all of your little churches will have united into one powerful Church of Niugini, using both the words of Christ and your own traditional spiritual knowledge. And maybe you will be sending missionaries out around the world, down to Australia, teaching us of the true words and how to sing again.'

Everybody laughed at the idea — but to me it was beginning to make sense. Europeans have taken the crown of Christianity unto themselves, used it up and lost its power. We mumble hymns of praise and snigger at the wisdom of prophets. Time for a vigorous new church. I might go to that one.

Kopi clicked his tongue and stood.

'Thank you for your stories Phil. But now we must say goodnight. We must climb the hill, for all those beautiful women are waiting.'

Launi and Pauline cheered their exit, wishing the predators luck, and I breathed easier. Kopi had enjoyed the stories, but his life was his own. My spell was broken and he was off to dance the night away.

Massi village lies just to the east of Goroka on the road out of town to Mount Hagen. It is a long ribbon of a village that stretches from the central highway up a ridge towards the top of the mountain. At the top, in cold, wet rainforest, lies the world famous Gahavasuka National Park. The nation's best collection of orchids and rhododendrons, and a wilderness park. The walk from the centre of Goroka to the top of the mountain is a walk through time to the top of the world.

Leaving the smorgasbord of delights at the Bird of Paradise hotel you pass the artefact market outside the government buildings, the police station and courthouse on the right (with its carpark crowded with families of offenders) and the airport on the left — jet aeroplanes and computerised offices. Down the hill is the wonderful fresh food market. Traditional foods and new, sweet potatoes and avocado, strawberries and pitpit, ginger and greens. Hundreds of people buying and selling, bartering, yelling. Across the road, behind the rugby oval/cricket pitch is the magnificent Raun Raun Theatre. Beneath its soaring roof of grass is a wonderfully dynamic performance space, but keep walking; still a long way to go. Past the shops and some gardens, down the hill and through the cutting to the bridge. Brown-coffee water rapidly running over rocks. The betel market. Nuts and pepper and lime for sale, games of chance, win a chicken. Can I get you anything masta?

When you continue up the hill don't stop just over the bridge or someone is bound to tell the gruesome story of a shocking car accident which once happened. Keep climbing past the new teachers' college houses, and the cemetery. When you see the primary school on the left as you climb out from the river valley, already sweating profusely, you turn right. There is a big sign to the national park.

Stop and have a good look around if you haven't done so already. You are surrounded by mountains. Keep walking up the ridge through the village. Many of the first houses you see are modern, some of cheap construction, some brick and tile. The higher you walk the less you will see of the new stuff. People get poorer and more traditional the further you walk up the hills. More and more thatched roundhouses are seen in their friendly clumps. Come early in the morning and you will see them steaming in the cold air as the smoke from their fires wafts through the thatching.

Wherever you walk, the people are polite and welcoming. They may ask too many questions — you go where? — but only out of friendly interest. The village council made a decision that travellers using the road to reach the park should receive the utmost courtesy. Reflecting on the terrible negative image that PNG receives in the world's press, they determined that in their village at least the world would see civilised behaviour. I have always felt very safe in Massi.

Towards the park the roundhouse clumps become smaller and are surrounded by pristine gardens. Then they disappear and you enter the rainforest. Black birds of paradise chortle-call and dip and soar through the shadows. Water drips, ferns uncurl, greenery grows.

The entrance to the park is a little English surprise of flowerbeds and stands of flowering bushes. There are displays of rare and beautiful orchids and vistas of rhododendrons which steal the mountain light and send it back out coloured.

Climb further, exhausted now, up narrow mountain tracks cut skilfully into the mud. The jungle closes in. There is no sign of humanity. This is the home of Nakombi, strange half man/half spirit. His cave is somewhere on the other side of the mountain, but he's here. You can feel him.

Suddenly the rainforest gives way to a breathtaking view right down the valley to Goroka in the far distance. A plane comes over a distant ridge and banks and turns and disappears into all the other silver sunflashes of town. A tiny town surrounded by vast greenery and mountains. Here lies Niugini. Drink it in.

During this stay in Massi village I had the pleasure of getting to know Kopsi, the head botanist of the park. He was one of those rare human beings with the perfect job. His home village was at the top of the ridge and he could walk to work in the mornings through the rainforest. He had travelled the length and breadth of PNG collecting examples of rare orchids. Noting their altitude and position in relation to the sun, he was able to successfully transplant them in his gardens. He had rescued endangered specimens from in front of bulldozers in Bougainville, or so the story goes. He was a lucky, happy, generous and hard working man.

Around that time he was the lucky recipient of the services of an Australian volunteer. This bloke, let's call him Ian, was an expert in road erosion control. He had come to PNG for six months to help the park avoid environmental damage wrought by increased traffic. An honourable challenge.

Before leaving Australia Ian had taken the wise step of gaining advice. He visited an old New Guinea hand, a retired Australian who had worked for many years in PNG. The knowing old fellow advised Ian to become an 'action man' in order to win the respect of the locals. An action man is someone who is seen to be doing things, who makes a difference. It is generally expected that white experts on relatively high wages will do just that. The fact that Ian was a volunteer on subsistence wages would not have been understood. All white people are regarded as rich in PNG. So Ian needed to prove himself by working hard and taking decisive action. He needed to make an obvious difference fairly quickly. Or so he was led to believe.

Our Aussie's job was principally to advise on environ-mentally sustainable construction techniques for roads and walking tracks throughout the park. As a professional greenie, he was well suited to the task. His big mistake, however, was to become an action man too quickly.

To his mind the driveway entrance to the park looked too much like an English country garden. The neat rhododendron and orchid beds rankled him. This was the entrance to a superb wilderness area and he felt it should look more rugged. The local people had no idea what he was talking about and equivocated. Flower lovers from around the world came to see the wonderful display, and for them the entrance gardens were not incongruous in the slightest. Everybody loved them the way they were but nobody made that really clear to Ian.

One day he became tired of the seemingly constant meetings and consultations necessary to get anything done. So he took the advice of his Australian mentor and became Action Man. With a large spade and wheelbarrow he attacked the flower gardens and redesigned the entrance-way to highlight the rainforest surrounds. He worked like a man possessed and the change was profound.

A group of angry men came to see me at Launi's hut that night. They knew I was Kopsi's friend and they wanted to know what to do about the Australian interloper. They said Kopsi had been found in the mud of his orchid garden in tears, scrabbling through the ruins trying to find living orchids. His babies. Some were very rare, and the man was in despair. They told the whole story in hushed and brittle tones, and asked what should be done. 'There are some of us in the mountain who believe we should just push him off a ridge. Kill him. Our brother has been crying and honour is at stake.'

I went to see the idiot the next morning and he made the right apologies and started to pull his head in. He ended up doing a good job. Everyone began to like him once he had accepted that what he thought was good for the people might not be what they wanted at all. It is a lesson all expert expats must learn.

The Henganofi Convention

Towards the end of our rehearsal time in the village, the country's big men came to Goroka. A national election campaign was beginning and the Pangu Party, the Prime Minister's party, was holding a pre-election convention in the Eastern Highlands. A former Pangu Party cabinet minister lived in our village, and he invited Launi and I to attend as his guests. Launi was not too keen but I fancied a ticket to a political convention in the wilds of PNG. It had Hunter S Thompson written all over it. Launi organised for his cousin Rodney to take me.

The night before the convention I sat beside a village fire and got wonderfully pissed in preparation for my sortie into Hunter S territory. The mix of alcohol, surreal company (Highland warriors) and smoky mountain air concocted an intense sense of the weird. We laughed and drank loudly. When I staggered away to piss I saw that thin clouds had filled the valley and crept up the ridges like giant spider webs. Later we spat the pips of a pungent red fruit into the fire. When I crawled into my sleeping bag I was wired. Unable to sleep I fitfully replayed scenes from *Fear and Loathing in Las Vegas* and resolved to keep playing the Hunter S game in the morning — I'd get involved and push my way to the front.

A horn honked mournfully through the chilly mountain mists and I woke groggily. Prime Minister Namilau's jet was due in Goroka in a short time and we would have to move fast to join the official welcome. I shook my fuzzy head and struggled out of my warm sleeping bag and into the best clothes I could find in the dim light of the roundhouse. But by the time I staggered out of the door and into the strawberry field all that remained of my host was diesel fumes and the echo of his contempt for young people who cannot get out of bed. Chastened, Rodney and I walked rapidly down the mountain, the tropical sun washing our nice clean clothes with sweat.

I was, of course, anxious to indulge in drugs, that being the true badge of a gonzo journalist, but all we could lay our hands on were betel nuts. Chewing and spitting with fervour, red gobs flying to the footpath, I try to convince myself that this crimson crud is giving me a mind-altering experience. Alas, whilst the strenuous walk is burning off the residue of last night's alcohol the buai does nothing for me. I am cold sober. Hunter S will not be impressed by Philip V.

By the time we stomp into Goroka the cavalcade has already completed its majestic sweep, bestowed its blessings and headed for the hills. The town seems unchanged by the big man's benevolence, humming and chattering as always. We tread the streets for half an hour trying to con a driver to join us in our journey to Convention City. We settle for a ride in a Public Motor Vehicle, huddling in a fifteen seat Toyota bus that hurls us around the mountains to Henganofi. Diesel fumes and Highland sweat mix liberally in the air and, as we pass by stunning mountain views and are passed by suicidal maniacs in four-wheel drives, my sense of reality is strangely heightened. When we arrive I leap from the bus, adrenalin charged, as high as the Owen Stanleys and gonzo ready.

The wandering crowd and barking loudspeakers lead us to the convention centre. It is a swamp — a flooded football field awash in mud with a half-heartedly decorated stage at one end. Most of the crowd huddles near the entrance on a semblance of dry land but I leave Rodney there and push forward through thousands of Highlanders, squelch across the open bog and enter the eight or nine rows of party faithful standing close to their leaders. I am one of the few wearing shoes. Obviously everyone else knew that ankle deep water would surround the PM. Perhaps it is a clever security measure.

The local member is trying desperately to convince the crowd that Pangu is the only hope for law and order and Highland's power and work and prosperity and the end to all hardship. Far more interesting is an ex-member of the party in an antique blue safari suit who moves amongst us in the crowd.

'Don't listen to these men. They are politicians, liars, here to steal your land and your money,' he shouts at us. 'You! Get back to your village, all of you go home. Leave these men. You mean nothing to them except your votes. Give them nothing. Go home!'

This is, of course, given in rapid fire pidgin, as is the speech from the podium. I'm enjoying myself trying to translate an exotic language into familiar electioneering. If I stop trying to understand the individual words, and just let the speech wash over me, the gobbledegook is punctuated by international politick-speak.

'Daa dee da dee da COMMODITY PRICES dum de dum INTERNATIONAL MONETARY FUND yum tum yum tum FREE TRADE POLICY la di da COALITION

PARTNERS tiddle eye po DEMOCRATIC PROCESS.' In PNG the bullshit is isolated into a foreign language.

The choir is to sing. Good, I love Highland singing. Bad, they have their backs to us. I hope the PM and his twenty flower-bedecked cronies on the stage enjoy the songs of praise. The thousands of us just hear the occasional high note and the continued preaching, far off now, of the blue safari suit. When he next yells 'Go back to your village!' we all wish we could. The power of the microphone has been broken, we become aware of our soggy feet and only the impending speech of the Prime Minister holds us in the mud.

I am very conscious of the power of the Big Man in this culture. In the village the rich and powerful businessmen are respected in spite of any wrong doings. Their bigness deserves respect no matter how they managed to rise above their fellows. Thus I was expecting a huge wave of admiration to greet the PM, the Biggest Man in the country. Yet as Rabbie Namalau takes the microphone there is no electric thrill, no pushing forward, no sense of occasion — just a spattering of applause from the few party faithful. Perhaps New Guineans are becoming as cynical about their pollies as we are in Australia.

Mr Namalau is not prize gonzo material. From up close he comes across as a very nice man, intelligent and polite. In slow, clear pidgin he joins every leader in the world in blaming poverty on commodity prices. He talks of post-Bougainville National Unity, of a mining-led recovery and of sharing mineral wealth with traditional landowners. He is reasonable and reassuring but here, with three thousand damp Highlanders surrounded by dramatic mountains, it is time for inspiration. The mud leaches our energy and we want passion.

I take a few notes and photos. This causes a little action

up on the podium where bored VIPs have spotted the whitefella and assume I must be a journalist. They pose and smile for me. The crowd opens up and politely waves me to the front. I get a couple of good shots, then become bored with the smiley Big Men on the stage. I turn my back on them to shoot the bizarrely dressed crowd and I'm the first to see it — a huge ugly black cloud trailing a heavy curtain of rain. People turn to see what I see and a low murmuring begins. Then in an instant a communal decision is mysteriously made and the organism which is the crowd splits into individuals and hurries away.

The Prime Minister just keeps talking. He ignores our calamity and drones on while his three thousand constituents turn to three hundred. Large drops of rain hit me and I run to the side of the stage for a little protection. The men on the covered stage, safe and dry, nod and smile. The PM keeps talking to an empty field, only thirty of us now listening.

Then lightning, thunder, a fierce squall which whips away the lunch marquee and sends me running through stinging rain, leaping large puddles and skiing across sheets of mud. I laugh and whoop for two hundred yards and then dash for shelter under a house. As I take cover the gutter bursts and showers us with water. I dive next door where I see bodies leaping through windows, vaguely aware that Rabbie is still rabbiting on. Panting with exertion I find myself in a long, dark room inhabited by twenty black strangers in violent, lawless New Guinea. Will they rob me of my camera and shoes? They look at me, I look at them.

Highland New Guineans can be a ferocious looking people. In Goroka I am protected by my connection with Massi village but here I am an unconnected stranger. I try not to show my fear. I stand dripping into the mud floor, as do my staring companions. We are all very wet. I pull off my shirt, wring out the water and put it back on again. The others grin and copy me. I feel great relief. We keep warm with silly jokes.

The gods turn off the rain and we emerge into sunshine and steaming mud. There is a traffic jam as VIP cars try to ferry their precious cargo from the stage to the hastily re-erected lunch marquee. The wet, muddy crowd stares into the cars as dry, clean men wave back, looking uncomfortable in their comfort.

Rodney finds me and we are spotted by our host from the village. He waves us past security, across more mud and into the hastily re-erected tent, apologising all the way for this farce of a convention.

'We should be talking amongst ourselves about policy, not haranguing crowds,' he confesses. I politely agree, then stop, stunned at the view of the tables groaning under the weight of a mountain of food. It's Rabelais meets the Country Women's Association. Hunks of meat and sticky-sweet things and salads and taro/kumu slice. The feast stares at the bedraggled guests. We stare back. We wait and wait and start to steam. The hot food stops steaming, but nobody steps forward to eat.

Eventually an embarrassed official arrives clutching a huge bag of plastic forks and paper plates. So that was the hold up. I don't know why we didn't just eat with our fingers and hands.

'The Prime Minister will now serve himself, followed by the Premier of the Eastern Highlands Province and our other special guests,' we are informed by a pompous petty official. 'You may then join in, forming an orderly line moving in one direction. This direction,' he indicates with a nod.

Mr Namalau chooses his morsels daintily, chatting briefly with the cotton frocked catering ladies. These women have the same build, the same dress sense, the same expressions as their rural Australian sisters who prepare food for similar occasions. A mixture of hard toil and sugar and Jesus has made them seem identical except for the colour of their skin. As I stare at this bizarre cross-cultural twinning the line grows bigger and bigger. I hastily hop aboard.

Soon people are passing out of the marquee with the most incredibly stacked paper plates the world has ever seen. Some are two feet high towers of sustenance — coleslaw on sponge cake, slabs of fatty meat decked with doughnuts covered in drumsticks, salad rolls, cream buns, garden greens and tinned fish rice. The PM must be feeling very foolish with such a little pile of food.

I take a fair whack myself, so as not to lose face, although I stick to the savouries (cross-cultural experiments have their limits). As I stack my plate the official starts yelling loudly. 'There are people here who do not have to be here. If you are not supposed to be here go away.'

Everybody stops and looks around for the naughty people who have gatecrashed, then shrug their shoulders at such temerity and turn back to the food. Not one person leaves.

As I walk into the sun to eat the orderly line begins to fracture as more and more people appear. Bodies leap over fences and emerge from behind walls. The security men run in to grab their share of food before it is all gone. Children rush in between legs and suddenly all sense of order is gone. Tables disappear beneath the crowd.

'Somewhere in there is the head of state,' I think. 'Where's the security? Where's the tear gas? Where's the PM?'

Within seconds the storming of the tables is over and not a morsel remains. The PM is left standing in the middle of the space. Perhaps he dived in to the horde to grab the last cream doughnut. If so, it was a sublime political move, because he has now taken centre stage for his final chat to the people. I listen to more promises and platitudes as I share my bounty with half a dozen kids. Everyone is sharing the food from their piled high plates, and everybody gets a feed.

I hitch a ride home on the back of a truck. I am returning to Massi well fed, happy and sober — an obvious failure as a gonzo journalist. As I gasp at the dramatic beauty of the ridges and valleys, and the suicidal fanatics overtaking us on the crest of hills, I ponder on the coming elections. Many people, here and overseas, fear bloodshed with homemade guns and tribal violence. I am not so sure. Today I have seen healthy cynicism deflect the bullshit and a prime minister walk unscathed from a hungry mob. Politicians and their cargo cult promises are losing their potency. If we are lucky the biggest fights will be over the last cream bun.

Wantoks

The creation of our second work to tour PNG was not easy. I had arrived with a one-man show which portrayed my experiences of Niugini. A lot of it was not suited to touring the country it described. The descriptions of exotic cultures that so thrilled Australian audiences were of little interest here and I was embarrassed by some of my observations. They seemed a little voyeuristic in situ. Not only that, the country had changed considerably over the decade since I had last visited and I needed to update. Choosing to perform in schools and communities further eroded my stock of material — several scenes needed censoring and subtle work needed rejigging.

My principal problem however was that Launi was proving incredibly shy. He was not sure that he wanted to act the idiot again on stage. His new role as community leader required a certain dignity that sat awkwardly with stage comedy. I had a hard time getting him going, but after a couple of weeks he finally clicked back in to the fun of performance.

We edited my Wantok show down to twenty minutes or so of fast and funny scenes of a whitefella struggling with the vagaries of PNG. These were balanced by solo work from Launi recounting his experiences in Australia.

His mime about the exotic smell of Australian women was particularly funny. His observations of the place of our old people were sad and enlightening.

We also needed scenes that involved us both. While rehearsing I remembered the time we fought over the red sports car during my first trip and our recent argument over our disappointment in each other. Recalling the dynamic effect these conflicts had on others I suggested we make a scene in the play in which we fight each other. There is something potent about a white man and a black man attacking each other in public. We based the new scene on the red sports car affair.

We performed the play to six thousand people of all walks of life. At a school in the freezing badlands of Chimbu we had to play sport with the students to become warm enough to perform. In Madang I had to recover in hospital after a hellish drive across the mountains suffering from bad water which caused violent shitting and vomiting attacks. In Port Moresby the glitterati attended along with the Australian High Commissioner. All the performances were packed with people and generated a gratifying degree of laughter and debate.

The symbolism of a white man and a black man working so well together was very potent. With Australia and PNG working so closely in many areas the audience could read our onstage relationship in many ways. The fact that we worked together so well was seen as an encouraging sign for the future of our national relationships.

The fight scene had the most dramatic effect. When we really went for each other the audience was on the edge of their seats. It was like gladiatorial combat. They were almost embarrassed to be watching but couldn't take their eyes off us. After the dangerous climax, in which we almost came to blows, the scene evolved into one of mutual understanding. Our friendship endured and strengthened as a result of the quarrel. The audience breathed again and applauded our breakthrough. This occurred wherever we performed, whether it was in villages, schools or universities. It was the most talked about aspect of the show. We were obviously dealing with a critical subject.

The people of PNG and the western world have a love/hate relationship. Melanesian ways and capitalism are fundamentally different. Extended and nuclear families are poles apart. Yet we live in the same shrinking world and must deal with one another. Often we deal within the limits of diplomacy, burying our passions and fears beneath a veneer of smiles and handshakes. Perhaps in our play Launi and I represented symbolic exemplars of our differing cultures, and broke those diplomatic and social taboos with our violent argument. The fight scene demonstrated that forceful argument need not be destructive, and that a mature relationship includes the capacity to differ passionately. We cleared the air, talked straight and got to the bottom of our conflict. It was dangerous and scary, but truthful and effective. It proved the deep strength of our relationship, and I think offered new insight into communication between black and white.

I have often observed the strange way we relate to others of another culture. I have observed ratbag Australians in PNG behaving with polite niceties they would never use at home. Papua New Guineans control their bubbling passions when communicating with us. We have learnt to communicate within the universal doctrines of western diplomacy — keep the emotions in check, stay reserved, polite and good humoured. At times this works wonders, but it is not the only way. Sometimes westerners could usefully bend a bit in the other direction and respect the force of passion within other cultures. Sometimes we too should let our feelings be clear and sport with our companions. In other cultures a fight can clear the air; passion and strength can win respect, an understanding of fears and hurt feelings can create lifelong friendships. We can't always expect everyone else to follow our rules. Sometimes we too should walk on the wild side. It is quite refreshing.

This trip to PNG had been very successful in terms of cultural exchange, but I was aware of the absence of that sense of magic I had experienced on my first visit. The old shaman Poppa Doiki was dying and the country was developing and moving into the future. The old ways were not for me to see on this trip, and I didn't look for them.

I returned to Australia determined to set my career alight but instead walked into gloom. I picked up Lynn and the kids in New South Wales and we returned to Western Australia, to the most isolated city in the world. It was not a joyful homecoming. As we drove across the desert and into the city and into the street where our little house waited, there was a building of dread. We didn't want to be there. Life was somewhere else. We went through the motions of getting jobs and setting up a home, but our hearts weren't in it.

And then came an offer from Madang, on the north coast of PNG. Come and set up a theatre company, come and run culture and tourism projects throughout the province. My parents were upset. We had just got back from years away in the north and east and now we contemplated taking their grandchildren into savage lands.

Lynn and I thought long and hard and realised that we had to go. If we refused the offer and life continued to be uninspiring we would never forgive ourselves. Off we went, back to the jungle, the mosquitoes and rascals, the mountains and drums. I packed the necklace up tightly and took it with me. Deep in my heart I knew it was time to return the old snake to the mountains of home. I think it agreed with me.

Tropical Shores and Sores

We flew into Madang at sunset, out of the mountains and around the bay. Lights from fishing canoes rimmed the shore and fires burned on hillsides. We were greeted as VIPs in the tin shed where the baggage is collected. They lowered frangipani necklaces onto our necks and shook our hands. The air was wet with heat. We all smiled nervously and wondered what we had got ourselves into. I was given the keys to my work vehicle, a powerful, luxurious four-wheel drive, the best car I had ever had. We drove through the grasses and squatter camps on the way to town, past coconut groves and trade stores and knots of mysterious people. The kids stared in wonder at their new home. We drove past our prospective house, which was built on stilts overlooking the ocean. A candle was burning and tatty curtains blew in the breeze. The promised renovation hadn't taken place and someone was living there. We went to a hotel for two free nights of luxury and wondered what would become of us.

Madang is a fecund wonderland where even the mountains grow and the seabed rises. It is a young steep land of fractured valleys and islands. Volcanoes still thrust and pump, earthquakes rattle and tidal waves flatten. There are hundreds of islands, long ribbons of tropical coastlines, a massive river and an extraordinarily high and rugged central core dotted with fertile valleys. There are hundreds of unique languages and thousands of village cultures. The rainforests are unsurpassed, the reefs are among the world's best. And I was the new Executive Director of the Madang Visitors and Cultural Bureau.

What a title! What a job! I worked for an instrumentality of the Provincial Government of Madang. Amongst my responsibilities I was to: form a new Provincial Theatre Company, restructure and run a museum and artefact shop, develop locally owned tourism projects, promote Madang throughout PNG and overseas, organise singsing groups for special occasions, host international visitors, liaise with landowners for prime tourism sites, develop a tour guide accreditation and raise the status of Madang culture in general. I was also expected to train locals and attract talent so that when I left, in three years time, managers from Madang could take over.

Within days of our arrival, however, I discovered that the organisation was $150,000 in debt. After my initial anger died down I realised that all I could do was say no to most requests for help and just set up a few pilot projects whilst balancing the books. Later I realised that it was a godsend. I was forced to focus on only a few things at a time instead of going nuts trying to help everyone.

I thought about trading in the car I had for a cheaper one. Although it was a beauty, I was prepared to let it go. But that little sacrifice became unnecessary when I discovered it had been bought duty free and we had to hold on to it for three years or pay the tax. I had no money to spend on the job, but I had a lovely car. Oh New Guinea!

Remembering the lesson of the orchid garden of

Gahavasuka, I knew that whilst I had to be an action man I also needed to move slowly and carefully. At first this balance seems impossible, but then you see the safe things that can be done and recognise the contentious jobs to avoid. I had, for instance, been given a file containing applications from seventeen villages for assistance in building a village guest lodge. I knew that if I chose to help one the other sixteen would be upset with me. It was too early to make enemies so I hid the file for a while.

As a whitefella my first act was to appoint a cultural adviser. I found Simon, an actor, dancer and director. He was introduced to me as a possible director for the theatre and I offered him the job. It would take a couple of months to get the new theatre company moving, but I needed help immediately. Simon was able to sit in on meetings and advise me of the undercurrents, politics and meanings that I couldn't hope to pick up. He advised me early on not to make promises to anyone, and helped me to win over some problematic people.

One problem he couldn't help with was my housing. The promised house, which overlooked the sea and sat below the museum, had a squatter. She was the former executive director who had been sacked six months previously. There were counter claims about compensation and she refused to move. As a result the desperately needed renovations had not even been started. We were put up in a gloomy expat enclave behind the fabulous Mandang Resort Hotel whilst things were sorted out. It was not the style of housing we had come for. Lynn was fed up and I was furious. The board wanted to leave the mess for me to deal with. I refused.

The woman came from KarKar, volcanic home of 20,000 people just off the coast. I had no desire to be seen as the white bastard who stole their wantok's job and then threw her out of her house. I didn't want thousands of enemies before I started. I had to work with these people. We spent months in the compound while the politicians dithered. New Guinea takes its time.

There were six basic apartments in a row with a security man on the gate. The pool was green and the home of large toads. The rooms were small and hot ,and the views and neighbours gave no indication that we were in PNG.

A week or so after arriving we were invited to dinner by a group of expatriate neighbours. It soon became clear that it was an informal orientation for us into the vagaries of Papua New Guinea. I was naughty and didn't tell anyone that I was no stranger to PNG. Instead I sat back and listened to the warnings given out to newcomers. Some of the advice was valid, but a lot displayed a dismaying ignorance. I began to voice another opinion.

'Well you try whatever you like Phil,' our host concluded. 'But don't forget the basic fundamental truth that you can never actually trust these people.'

'I have to trust them.'

'Well you can't, not completely. You think they're all right, but they'll always bugger you up in the end. You have to keep checking up on them.'

'Well that's my whole management strategy down the drain then. My companies work because I trust my colleagues.'

'You'll need a new strategy here,' was the doleful reply.

I went to work on Monday determined to prove them wrong. I immediately set up a petty cash system and instructed my staff how to use it. Everybody had access to the cash and the system would last as long as it was honoured. It lasted, and I received the most wonderful support from all of my workers. I trusted them completely, allowing them at times to sleep on the premises and even have friends visit. In response they looked after the museum and its gardens brilliantly. There was no pilfering. None of our valuable carvings disappeared. I gave them the courtesy of acknowledging that they could be honest, and they replied with honour.

To be seen as Action Man I decided to make a big deal of reopening the museum complex. This was in a quite beautiful, soaring building set amongst gardens overlooking the ocean. However the collection was unclassified, unlisted and unloved. Most of the ancient artefacts were in a big pile on the floor. With help from local businesses we built new display cases and invited local elders to visit the museum to identify objects of importance. Our displays began to make sense, and I wrote out the stories of fascinating carvings or photographs as told by the old people who visited. This won me admiration. Within a day of hearing a new story we would type and print it out on a card in English and pidgin and put it on the walls. This was Action Man at work, and it demonstrated cultural respect as well. My stocks began to rise.

There was a 1920s photo of two strapping brothers from Siar Village, which is close to Madang. An old man from Siar instantly recognised the two young men, and told their story. One day a crippled woman arrived on a boat from KarKar Island, the volcanic massif that dominates the horizon. She pulled herself along the beach with her hands, her useless shrivelled legs leaving strange tracks on the beach. She was tiny yet determined. She had run away from abuse and the lack of a future, and hoped to find a husband and a life on the mainland. The people of Siar were amazed by this deformed woman who demonstrated such courage. One man stepped forward and offered to marry her and take her into his household.

She bore him, and the village, two strong and vigorous boys who grew to become the biggest, strongest men on the coast. She lived a full and fruitful life, and her boys kept the village protected and won the community great esteem. What a wonderful story for the wall of a museum, a story from which anyone, villager or tourist, might draw inspiration.

Lynn and I planned an early trip up to Goroka to visit my family and friends in Massi village. The community was anxious to meet my wife and kids and we wanted to drive across the mountains and down the valleys of what must be one of the world's great drives. A rugged, muddy haul across one mountain range, then a steep, searing, soaring climb out of the Markham valley and into the Highlands. It is six to eight hours of vibrantly changing landscape and culture, an intoxicating mix of danger and beauty. Before embarking I called Launi to see if he needed anything from the coast. He asked us to buy some sago from the markets for Pauline as she missed her Sepik staples. I told him I was bringing the necklace home.

'Why did you bring that thing back?' he growled.

'Because it seemed like the right time. Because you said it would come back to Niugini when the time was right,' I answered.

'It is not the right time,' he instructed. 'Leave it in Madang. Do not bring it home.'

'Okay, it's your necklace.'

'No, it's yours,' he replied mysteriously. 'But leave it there for now.'

Despite not having my protective necklace draped around the gear stick where it usually travelled, and a recent upsurge in rascal hold-ups, we had a trouble-free trip to Goroka.

All the time we were there Launi would not talk about my magic keepsake. He just shook his head negatively whenever I broached the subject. I told him one night about my experience of the cave that breathed. I think I had hoped that by discussing such matters I might be able to twist the conversation round to the necklace, but he gave me no chance. In fact, my story really distressed him. Like Paul, he seemed jealous of my experience of the spirits. He told me of a time when he needed magic protection for his Australian wife in Goroka and an old shaman had given him special leaves to ring his house. Later he asked the old man for help in getting back in touch with his power.

The old man had led him for hours through jungle and hillsides. It poured with rain and in the darkness the magician disappeared. Launi sat all night sheltering under big leaves. He was angry and resentful and filled the hours cursing or thinking of food for his belly. At dawn the old man returned, looked at him disdainfully and led him home. As Launi left the grove he turned to look at the tree he had sheltered under. Only then did he recognise the leaves. He had spent the night beneath his people's sacred tree and not noticed. This had confirmed in his mind that his spirit was lost or damaged and this made him angry at the apparent ease of my own experiences. I tried to console him. My moments of contact, I argued, were serendipitous. At best I had a knack of being in the right place at the right time. Unlike him I had no heritage of magic. Perhaps he tried too hard, I suggested. I counselled patience, convinced that his inherited powers would still be intact, but he didn't want to know. I left him steaming and went to bed.

Apart from that we had a lovely time in the village. We introduced cricket to Massi, learnt some new games ourselves, and Lynn and Pauline fell in love, the two wives of the doppelgangers. Until now the kids had generally found visiting villages a bit of an ordeal. In each new community hordes of strangers wanted to hold and carry the cute little white children. It was different in Massi. In some exotic way it felt like home. The kids in the village were my kids' cousins and nephews. They weren't treated as strangers, so it was more fun. Unfortunately the infections that were to dog our life began to flare up, and Ren developed dreadful earache and we returned to the coast early.

Back home in Madang I wrapped the necklace back around my gear stick again and it travelled everywhere with me. It was my good luck charm. I felt fairly safe in town; I had plenty of friends looking after me. It was on the road that I felt vulnerable. The surfaces are muddy and treacherous, the other drivers unpredictable.

Late one night, on the way home from visiting friends, we drove through the squatter-camp district in a thick mist. As we came around a bend the road was suddenly full of people fighting. I hit the brakes and dropped gears in a frantic attempt to stop before I entered the throng. The kids were asleep on the back seat, Lynn alongside, as we slid into the crowd. Suddenly an old man jumped in front of us and yelled a command. The fight stopped, and they cleared the road. He waved us through and, as we passed, the thirty or so protagonists jumped back into the fray. We drove through a very sticky situation, in our flash car, without a scratch. The necklace seemed to wink at me in the moonlight.

Towards the end of the dry season (though it still rained

most nights) a young man made his way from the northern mountains to my office. When I first saw Moyang I was struck by his beauty and healthy strength. He was shy, but he had purpose. When he said he had come about starting a village lodge I remembered the file I had hidden and my instinct was to show him the door. Luckily I asked some questions first, and when I realised that they had already built the lodge and he did not seek money I welcomed him into my office.

He told me of Salemben village and its beautiful mountain ridge, and of the threat to their magnificent rainforests. Malaysian loggers were moving in to the neighbouring coast and his people feared for their land. There are many such stories in PNG. Moyang explained that his village of Salemben had received nothing but promises since Independence. Now neighbouring communities, desperate for development and urged on by frustrated youth, were actively seeking forestry contracts for the sake of the work, roads and health centres they promised to bring. The people of Salemben, however, are travellers and they had seen the short-term gains and long-term destruction that logging brings. They feared for their land and the spirits who live within it.

Moyang told me of a recent tragedy. A young woman had died in childbirth, along with her baby, yet had the village owned a radiotransmitter an emergency helicopter could have saved both lives. The poverty of the people became an issue once again, and the young people had begun to agitate for change. After a long and dynamic village meeting the elders had decided that tourism, and not logging, would be the saviour of the people. They had built a lodge and sent Moyang to town to ask me to send tourists.

We looked at my map on the wall, and I realised that it

was no easy trip to get to Salemben. A long drive and a long hike were involved.

'What do you have to tempt travellers to journey so far? What is there to see?' I inquired of the young man.

'The Cliffs of Henespe,' he proudly answered. 'The cliffs are deep in the jungle, and they are tall and covered in dripping water, ferns and flowers. They are very beautiful. Amongst the rocks lies the canoe of Kilibob. It is the place where he first landed on the mainland. The cliffs are our masali place.'

Masali place, Kilibob's canoe. I shuddered with the realisation that Moyang was talking about walking tourists through a sacred site. Kilibob and his brother Manub are the creation brothers of the Madang coast. A masali place is taboo for all but the initiated.

'Do your elders agree with what you are suggesting?' I asked.

'Yes.'

'Are you sure?'

'Yes.'

I was not sure at all. It seemed wrong to open sacred places to tourists.

'Do your elders understand what it means to have strangers walking in your Masali place?'

'Yes, but you wouldn't ...'

'I wouldn't what?' I asked, trying to pull the thought from him.

'You wouldn't understand.'

'Because I am a white man?'

Moyang nodded. I smiled. 'Try me,' I implored.

'After we had the meeting my father and my uncle, both old and important men, chewed some roots and went to sleep to dream the answer to our problems. In the morning they came together. Both had dreamed a new dream, a dream they called the Keki dream, and it showed white strangers walking around the cliffs, and the spirits were happy. That is why we built the lodge. We think that if we show people our forests and masali place they will help us to protect them. We think that if the loggers ever try to enter our borders, or a corrupt government tries to give them a licence for our trees, then friends from overseas who know Salemben will come to our help.'

I couldn't fault the logic. I was no longer worried about the breaking of taboo or endangering of the sacred. It was a new dreaming now. It was in the hands of the gods. I smiled as I suddenly realised that I was being offered a classic 1990s adventure, the chance to help save a rainforest. Moyang smiled back.

'So will you come?' he asked. 'You yourself must see if we are worthy. That is all I have come to ask. Will you come and visit Salemben?'

I thought for a few seconds, then asked, 'Can I bring my family?'

His face blossomed into what I call a laugh-grin. It is not a state you often see on an Englishman, which is probably why we don't have a word for it. It is a smile of joy and accomplishment which dominates the face, shining through the eyes and teeth and cheeks. I repeated the question.

'Can I bring my family?'

'Oh yes, Mr Thomson ...'

'Phil'

More laugh-grin.

'Phil,' he corrected. 'Everyone will love it if your family comes'.

'We can't come for at least eight weeks.'

'It may be getting very wet by then.'

'I have to open the museum, the theatre … I can't … shall we make it later, next dry season.'

'Come as soon as you can. Leave a message on the radio and I will come back down to guide you.'

The government radio station was the prime form of communication in the rugged hinterland. Every village boasted at least one transistor radio, and messages invariably got through to the required individual. I promised to give him ample warning of our first available departure dates.

Simon had been sitting in my hot, dark office easing the discussion between Moyang and me. Moyang spoke English remarkably well, but Simon had become involved with translating concepts of myth and dreaming. He was there, as always, doing his job of ensuring that there were no cross-cultural misunderstandings. He had become more involved in this discussion than most. The idea of visiting new territory was exciting; the story of the Keki dreaming had inspired him as well.

'Can I come too?' asked Simon.

'Of course my brother. You are welcome to my village. We need your help too.'

We all laugh-grinned together, and Moyang left.

'Did you like him?' I asked Simon.

'Yes. Very much. You know he will go home and tell them all you are coming. They will be expecting you.'

'I know. I made a commitment. I want to go. It's what I'm here for. I didn't come to New Guinea to live in this hot building. I came to go out there. Grab your diary. Let's sort this out. When is the earliest we can go?'

We were excited and tried to rearrange dates so we could go earlier, but I was right the first time. Eight weeks until the first chance we'd get. We put it boldly into the diary, and then I went home to ask Lynn how she felt about us taking the kids up a mountain track. She was ecstatic.

Around that time Ren came into my bedroom in the middle of the night.

'There was a spirit in my room,' he told me, more with interest than fear. 'I woke up as it moved through the room, and it spoke to me.'

'What did it say?'

'It said "You're all right boy, don't worry," and then it was gone.'

Most strange of all was that the boy wasn't worried. He remembered in the morning and swore it wasn't a dream, but it didn't freak him out. He accepted the existence of the spirit without question, and did what it said.

While the museum began to take shape Simon and I were auditioning actors to form Malabo Theatre. Malabo is the local term for the flying fox, an important god/spirit and inhabitant of the region. Late every afternoon the skies of Madang become black with wheeling malabo before they head out across the bay in search of the fruits of the season. It was a good name for the company.

There were a few tensions around the Madang theatre world. There were already two part-time companies, and both were miffed that a new ensemble was being funded. I was lobbied, befriended and attacked behind my back — just the same as anywhere else in the theatre industry. By holding open auditions, and having Simon (who was unaligned) as director, we managed to overcome the problems. Actors and dancers from both companies were keen for the new company and the promise of a regular wage. We started with a small ensemble of six, and the training and rehearsal began. One of the actors, James, was from the squatter Sepik community on the outskirts of town. Although he was born in Madang, and was a great dancer in the Madang style, I was criticised strongly for appointing a non-Madang performer. The culture of Madang had long suffered from the strength of the neighbouring Sepik cultures (particularly in terms of carving) and some locals were adamant that I should protect Madang culture at all costs. I thought that I should appoint the performers Simon and I felt were the strongest and most talented. We believed Madang culture would be best served by appointing the best team. I also found the anti-James sentiments to be verging on the racist. My argument and defence of James caused a few ripples, the first test of my position, but I stood by my man, and he repaid my support with some brilliant work.

I discovered that we were expected in some quarters to produce primarily English language tourist-friendly theatre that the hotels could purchase. I strongly rejected this as our prime objective, believing that good local dance drama would actually be of more interest to travellers than just another tourist dance ensemble. Simon and I also believed that the company needed to play to its own people first if it was to become an important cultural organisation. I stood up to the big men and held my ground and my supporters remained solid. I knew that the first performance was going to be watched with interest, and that it had better be good.

The first play was called Bird Hunt, and it began as a series of traditional dances, with strong drumming, about the hunt and killing of a bird of paradise. I suggested injecting a number of slapstick chase routines into the moment between the hunters spotting the bird and capturing it. These proved to be great fun to invent and audiences loved the humour. Simon was an excellent dancer, and his bird was so beautiful the death scene became tragic. A robust celebration of dance and music became necessary to send the folks home happy.

The first performance was in the gardens of the hotel of the chairman of my board. Peter Barter was a former Australian pilot who had made a fortune as an hotelier. Just before my arrival in PNG he had won an election to represent Madang in the National Parliament. He was the hardest working man I have ever met. He never left his office before ten pm and seemed to live on a diet of cigarettes and coffee. He was also the member of the board who had fought hardest against my appointment (he had wanted a local for the job, which was fair enough). This show was a big test.

Peter pretty well ignored us as we set up in his gardens. He was hosting a meeting of the PNG/Australia Business Council. He had wanted us to perform indoors where his guests were eating, but the ceiling was so low and the stage so tiny I had insisted we use the beautiful gardens instead. That added more tension, as did the thunderstorm that was heading in our direction. The diners seemed happy enough to come outside, and they loved the show. They cheered, clapped and hollered. Several times Peter was heard taking credit for the company, and when he shook my hand firmly I felt we had won the first test. As the audience wandered back indoors for dessert, large tropical raindrops began pelting the gardens and lightning and thunder played out their own performance. We packed up happily in the rain. The actors said that Malabo had held back the deluge until the show was finished.

The next trial was the big one. It was crucial that we win over the Provincial Government members. Naturally quite a few of them were concerned about an Australian being nominally in charge of Madang culture. We decided to hold a public opening of the newly remodelled museum, along with the official launch of Malabo, at the time of the next parliamentary sittings when all the rural members would be in town.

Unfortunately this was the very week Lynn had booked to visit Australia. Luckily, we had met Eva, a young Danish nurse who needed somewhere to stay, and offered her a room if she would mind the kids during my last frantic evenings of getting the museum ready. Before Lynn left Eva came around for dinner. She told us some great stories, with graphic emergency room descriptions of the victims of flying long-tom fish, which are attracted by lights and pierce the torsos of hapless fishermen with their sword-like nose spears.

Another tale concerned that magnificent drive from Goroka to Madang, which Eva experienced as a passenger in a crowded minibus. A bus driver heading in the other direction flagged them down and urged them not to continue on into the Valley of the Rascals. This was an infamous strip of Highland road between Kianantu and Henganofi, allegedly run by gun wielding, dope growing outlaws. A lot of vehicles get held up, although I have never had any trouble, and the bus which stopped Eva had just received a thorough going over, and the passengers were most unhappy. Eva's driver consulted with his customers and they decided to take the risk, reasoning that the rascals would not hang around for long once they had executed a hold-up.

The tension in the bus increased as they entered the notorious valley, and suddenly an old Highland woman tapped our friend on the shoulder. In rapid-fire pidgin she demanded the white woman's camera, which she proceeded to bury deep amongst the potatoes in her billum bag. A man called to Eva to give him her wallet, another wanted her sunglasses. In stunned bewilderment she handed everything over to the demanding, ferocious looking people. When the bus finally passed through the Hijack Valley without incident the passengers all relaxed and dug into their bags to return Eva's valuables. They had known the rascals would steal all her wealth but might leave their poor possessions alone. At some risk to themselves they had looked after their overseas guest. The fiercest looking people may have the kindest hearts.

The museum opened to great acclaim, although many of the politicians we had hoped to win over failed to turn up. Nevertheless the new displays and scintillating performance from Malabo passed muster with many leaders of the community. I was a success, and I felt the tension of the last few months leave my shoulders as I shook hands with well wishers.

Later that night I returned to a flat of sleeping children and Eva showered and went to bed. I took care of my ablutions, but was horrified when I had my goodnight piss. It streamed out of my dick bright red! My knees buckled with shock. After a few minutes to recover I hobbled upstairs to get a medical opinion. What luck to have a nurse under my roof.

I knocked on her bedroom door.

'Yes,' came an oddly plaintive reply.

'Can I come in?' I asked, quite reasonably in the circumstances.

'Um ... just a minute.' There was a scramble within the room for a few seconds, and then Eva called me in. I found the beautiful young woman sitting up on her bed covered from head to foot in sheets and assorted clothing, which she clutched to her body with a quiet desperation.

'Yes?' she asked.

'I need some advice.'

'Oh yes?'

'I've just been to the toilet and I pissed blood.'

She looked so relieved. She smiled and said a faint 'Thank God.'

I had been so distraught I had not considered that she might think my knock on the door a sinister sign that her host was a horny arsehole with an absent wife. Eva had travelled on local transport as a single woman in many areas of PNG, and stayed with lonely expat men in isolated places, and hadn't experienced trouble at any stage. She had been treated with courtesy and good will by whites and blacks throughout the country. After all these months of surviving PNG without so much as a bad pick-up line she now thought she had a rampant fuck-wit at her door desiring her body. In retrospect I can't think of a better line to deflate such apprehension than 'I've just been to the toilet, and I pissed blood.'

She relaxed and welcomed me into her room and convinced me not to worry. A little blood makes a lot of red, and I just had a common tropical bladder or kidney infection. Thanks to her ministrations I was able to sleep easily and the next day I picked up some antibiotics from the chemist and it all cleared up. Or so I thought.

Within a few weeks of the museum opening, the Provincial Government of Madang was sacked by the National Government. All the men I had worked so hard to impress with my good work were gone, replaced by an appointed administrator. I wasn't too worried at first as I knew the new man and got on well with him, but the factions disputed his appointment and he was sacked within a week.

His successor was a different kettle of flying fish. A

man I only knew by reputation. Most of the expatriates in town regarded him as a white-hater, and my local friends painted him as some sort of Robin Hood, a Mafioso-like character who did good work for the community but was backed by a gang of heavies who ensured his wishes came true. I was summoned to meet the new administrator.

He was a former national rugby player from the mountains of Madang, and was huge in girth and height. He towered above me, and did not offer me a seat. Instead he fired off a series of rapid questions concerning my work. He obviously believed that I was a friend of Peter Barter, his political enemy. He demanded to know why I was helping out the big hotels and why I wasn't helping the locals.

I explained that he was completely wrong about my activities. I had come into the job concerned about the effects of tourism on traditional culture and was committed to forging partnerships with the locals. I told him I had discovered that the hotels did not require my assistance apart from operating an accessible information bureau. I had focused on developing commercial pilot projects with locally owned lodge, trekking and cultural activities. I had answers to all of his questions, and a clear conscience, but he still scared the shit out of me.

Standing beneath this angry Big Man as he hurled his accusations and question, one single message loop was running through my brain, 'Don't show fear … don't show fear … don't show fear …'

I survived the inquisition. After ten minutes or so of grilling he visibly relaxed and indicated a chair for me to sit on. He acknowledged that I seemed to be doing what he wanted me to do and, from there on, we had a very constructive chat. We worked well with each other after that but if, as the Chinese believe, the kidneys are the repositories of suppressed fear, that morning must have filled them to bursting.

Life settled down briefly. We experienced a tropical Christmas and missed our family and friends. We tried to keep the kids out of water, which was impossible, and consequently spent our lives washing out ears and drying them. Keeping the kids strong and off antibiotics was difficult. I worked. Lynn didn't, which pissed the hell out of her because she had been promised stimulating employment. A change of National Government had changed the rules and it became illegal for her to work. She did not take well to the life of an expat wife. Thankfully it was soon time for the trip to Salemben.

Moyang came to town a few days early and we bought the supplies he suggested. We left early in the morning. The air was almost crisp. It was one of those rare moments when you can see right across the bay. Usually there is a grey-blue horizon and no sense of land, but after a rain, if the wind is still and the sky is clear, you see 16,000-foot mountains peering over the sea. They take your breath away. We turned our backs to the peaks and drove north, Lynn and I in the front, and Moyang, Simon and the kids squeezed in the back.

The North Coast Road is sealed, and runs past coconut and cocoa plantations, fishing villages and black beaches. The massive volcanic island of KarKar grows bigger as you approach the manic waters of the strait that separates KarKar from the mainland. The waters there surge in strange directions, and throw tantrums as they slap the rocks. Then the road bends inland, offering only sudden flashes of a blue-black ocean. In the heat of the day brown lines of plantation palms hung with giant staghorn ferns open to reveal seemingly empty villages. We spot soccer fields and buffalo carts full of children. We wave a lot. A giant dead python is stretched across the road. The North Coast Road is an easy, purring drive.

Then we turned off down a track and into the mud, then up into the mountains. Now we were working. Holding on and flexing bodies as we bounced through creeks and powered up rises. The car lapped it up, but I wasn't experienced driving in thick black mud. Eventually there came a passage I couldn't cross. To the left were granite boulders and giant trees, to the right a gently curving slipaway of grass that fell away to plummet down into the valley. The track was pitted with deep wheel tracks that scared me and threatened to pitch the car down the slope. The wheels spun. I reversed and tried again. The kids got upset, and everybody climbed out as I tried again to no avail. Moyang suggested that we drive back down the track to the village we had recently passed to get some help to push us through. Leaving the family on the mountainside I reversed and swung back.

We reached the village just as all of the men were leaving. They were painted up in war paint and carrying spears and bows. Moyang called across and they yelled back that they couldn't help. A tribal fight was being set up and every man was required. Often these are just shows of strength and spear rattling. If everything is roughly equal they choose not to fight. Too many people will get hurt and the paybacks can be endless. However if one side is undermanned they can be routed. Every initiate is therefore called to arms to avoid bloodshed.

Whilst this was being explained to me one of the warriors walked over to my car and put his head in the window. He spoke very good English.

'What's the matter mate? This car should be able to get through, it's a beauty.'

'I guess I don't really know how to drive it in the mud.'

'It's easy. You know the creek at the bottom of that rise?'

'Yeah.'

'Well you've got to gun it from there. Get up to third as you get to that bad bit, then drop it down to second and power on through. Go for it. Those ruts won't throw you out, they're too deep.'

I nodded and gave thanks. We powered away and through the creek, showering the windows with brown water. We charged up the hill screaming with exhilaration and bounced through the ruts and out the other side. A war-painted, spear-carrying warrior had taught me how to control a four-wheel drive. That's modern Papua New Guinea — the world's greatest repository of unique cultures and languages turns to master the modern.

The hills around us were turning into mountains, with rounded shapes replaced by vertical uplifts and jagged spars of jungle draped rocks. Higher and higher we drove, into the clouds and beyond. At the turn of a bend we looked down into a deep valley, but the track stuck to the spur and wound down a ridge until it came to an end in Sevan village. There we left the car with the local schoolteacher. Three of Moyang's cousins and his sister were in Sevan to meet us. They carried the food and gifts as we headed up the ridge towards Salemben. Within a hundred yards Nina was sitting on Moyang's shoulders. Ren managed the first long climb until he too was lifted onto a strong back. We slipped from the gardens into a deeply silent forest of white trees with prominent roots before the track moved higher and higher, crossing bubbling streams and opening up to distant forest vistas. At times we turned a corner to enter the forest itself, tall creeper covered trees shading the sun, the ground covered in ferns of wondrous variety, multicoloured leaves, bright flowers and strange fungi. Exotic birds called and butterflies hovered in sunbeams. Another bend in the track revealed the ocean where beyond the shore stood the remarkable volcano of Manum funnelling clouds into the sky.

It had been raining. Our boots became clogged in thick heavy mud. Two steps up, one slide back. When we slipped the hands of our guides would grab our arms, and their toes would dig into the mud, and we held fast. We skated across slippery logs above gushing rapids that spat down the mountainside, but always our hosts held us hard. We felt clumsy but secure. And when Moyang began to tire of carrying Nina, she clung to him. Until now, despite some Aboriginal friends in Australia, she had been a little wary of all the black people who surrounded her in PNG. Clinging to the shoulders of beautiful gentle Moyang her nervousness transformed to adoration.

After a couple of hours we came to a few houses perched below a ridge. We stopped for a few minutes rest as one of the men played out a message on the giant garamut slit-drum that lay in the grass. His drum talking echoed down the valley and across to the distant ridges. 'They know we are coming now,' said Moyang. 'Good, we must be close,' replied my aching feet. Oh no, it was 'clos to nau' all over again. For another hour we toiled as the track zigzagged up the side of the mountain. We were covered in sweat when we turned the last bend and looked down a long glade. The village was hidden behind a tall woven fence through which we heard the urgent drive of kundu drums.

Before the entrance to the village there was a newly erected bamboo pipe shower for us to use. Where a stream bubbled out from a crevice in the rocks and down the hillside a system of bamboo pipes on tripod legs reached out towards the track. From the end of the bamboo, nearly three metres in the air, spilt a continuous stream of sparkling mountain water. It took my breath away before my sweat. Cooled and cleaned we approached the gateway into the village. A large sign had been hung welcoming us to Salemben Village.

We waited as the drums got louder and the sound of stamping feet could be clearly heard. Then voices were yelling and people were running and suddenly the gate just disappeared. Dozens of hands just threw the woven wall away and we were ushered into the village. An old man who turned out to be Moyang's father grabbed my forearm. His wife grabbed Lynn. They guided us into the middle of the brightly costumed singsing group. Back and forth they danced, moving us slowly through the village, our eyes glistening with the passion of the welcome. It was only later that we realised that for fifteen minutes or so we had completely forgotten our kids. They were somewhere back in the noisy throng and we weren't worried at all.

We stopped at the other end of the village outside of the new lodge. Every man, woman and child filed past us in traditional clothes, heads adorned with brilliant birds of paradise, faces painted in vivid stripes, teeth flashing quick, nervous smiles of welcome. Each person offered a gift — necklaces, headbands, bags, bowls, weapons and pig tusks. By the end we looked like walking tourist shops draped from head to foot in artefacts. Only when the crowd dispersed were we fully able to appreciate the splendour of our surroundings. Salemben village was beautiful. Orchids and other flowers lined the paths and gardens, pristine huts and lawns sparkled in the mountain sun and all around lay the distant barriers of jungle covered mountains.

The lodge was a cosy stilt hut split into two rooms. Built of timber, bark and leaves it boasted a small verandah looking across the valley. The people had built us a shower room for private washing (icy mountain water carried up the hillside in bamboo pipebuckets), and a dining room. This was a small open room with a hand hewn wooden table and benches. The arms of the seats had flowers growing in them. The toilet was down a diabolically slippery mudpatch. Every ablution involved a mad slide down the hillside and a frantic grabbing for trees before you missed the dunny and plunged out of sight.

That evening we ate chicken soup, greens and taro, bananas, pitpit, tinned meat and onions, noodles and coconut rice. A feast for the hungry walkers. We were informed that we were the first white family ever to visit the village. In fact, except for a few missionaries from whom most people hid, we were the first whites in Salemben. We were certainly the first to be welcomed and fed in this fashion, and would be the first to visit the cliffs. I felt privileged and marvelled at the fact that though we were the first white family here, some of our hosts spoke perfect English, thanks to a mission education down on the coastal plain. The moon lit up the ridge and struggled to penetrate the dark valley below. I was exhausted, but happy to my core.

Before we retired the people came back to our lodge to conduct a simple Christian ceremony. Moyang had promised this, and I was wary. I feared the Bible bashing of the modern militant missionaries but need not have worried. This was a simple prayer and hymn praising the heavens and thanking God for the earth's beauty. Using local language and western music this simple ceremony was a reminder of the strong spirituality of Papua New Guineans and the ease with which they amalgamate new and traditional belief systems. It was a gift for us, and a gift for the gods. Amid such simple splendour and enthusiasm it was impossible not to join in and offer our own thanks to the heavens as well. Life is good.

The next morning we were fed a fruit and noodle breakfast as the singsing group performed alongside our personal restaurant. An old man clown would leave the dancers and run into our room to steal food and make the kids laugh. After a wash we followed the dancers down the track, heading for the Cliffs of Henespe.

The entire village seemed to be with us, including one boy, naked except for paint, who played the clown and ran ahead to surprise us by hanging in strange fashion from the trees. Our boots became mud-logged and heavy, so we took them off and our toes slurped through the black mud giving us much better traction. We left the main track, and then took an even smaller one through a grove of fungus covered trees before we reached a small hut on the edge of the forest. The local women and girls remained there to make lunch as Lynn and Nina prepared to be the first women to see the cliffs. The Keki dreaming had white women in it. They were supposed to come with the men and the boys. We left the track and bush-bashed.

Our naked feet dropped through layers of leaf, compacting the spongy mass into something firm enough to walk on. At first I worried about standing on ragged thorns or needles of bamboo, but as we danced down through the trees, immersed in a long snake of tribesmen, it was like walking on clouds. Soft and wet and very giving. Very occasionally a leech would fancy a calf, but a bush knife flicked it away before you were really aware of it. We climbed down near-vertical inclines, through mosses and ferns, sometimes sinking deeply into the forest litter. Birds, insects and frogs called out as these strangers entered their peaceful paradise.

The cliffs loomed above us in the jungle gloom. Covered in creepers and mosses and overhung with trees it was hard to get a clear perspective. We followed the base of the cliffs looking up into the water droplets which spilled from the top. Our hosts spotted a baby bird in a nest and wanted us to see it, but try as we might we could see no bird. They insisted it was there but then changed their minds and hurried us on. There was a silence.

'What the hell was that about?' I whispered to Moyang.

'They wanted you to see the little bird. Then when you couldn't see it they realised that it was a spirit bird and not for you to see.'

Kilibob's boat prow, the most sacred part of the cliffs, rose mightily from the jungle floor. It did look like a boat, a limestone boat that had sat in the forest for eons. There must have been a huge flood to deliver it here at the top of a mountain. A Melanesian Noah. We marvelled at the tropical ark and then wandered back to the hut for lunch. On the way Moyang told us that he and several other men had just seen the white witch of the forest. This white female deity lives in the trees, and she spat on them.

'Does this mean we are unwelcome?' I asked.

'No. She spits when she is pleased.'

We ate lunch on the ridge above the sacred valley and I joined the men to smoke a huge cigar of local tobacco wrapped in newspaper. It blew my head apart. As it spun I sat and told a story I had heard in Goroka. When the missionaries arrived in PNG they discovered a lost people desperate for the Bible. Never before, anywhere in the world, had pagans received the word with such enthusiasm. Wherever the missionaries roamed the people would come out from the trees with open hands pleading for Bibles. 'Give me Bible, masta. Give me Bible'. The word was sent back to Europe and boatloads and planeloads of the good book were delivered into the jungles. Long lines of carriers would follow the priests up rivers and valleys and along the ridges, carting thousands of sacred books. And everywhere the people flocked to accept them. It turned out that Bible paper made the best rolling paper for cigarettes. I don't know if the story is true, but I hope it is. It has a delicious irony. My friends in Salemben, sitting high above their sacred cliffs, certainly enjoyed the yarn. They laughed so much they slapped themselves.

That night, after feasting on fresh avocados, tomatoes and fruits, tinned meat and rice, we sat in our little dining room and listened to stories. Moyang's people were coastal people who had moved high up into the ridge country. Their land ran up to the massive wall of mountains to their south. They were the highest of the salt-water people. The Highlanders to their north, ten minutes by plane, were from a different land. In the old days they treated each other as subhuman. Or so the stories went.

Our hosts wanted to know about Australia. Like everybody else in PNG they took it for granted that we lived in a state of beatitude. We managed to convince them that there is poverty and misery of sorts in every land. We insisted that their village seemed to us to be one of the richest places in the world. They liked that; it was good for strangers to confirm their blessings.

The next morning we walked around to see everyone's houses and pets, and then gathered our belongings as another singing group formed to escort us out of the village. The costumes they wore were extraordinary. The warriors had coconut masks, a perforated painted shell over each eye, and pig tusks clasped in their teeth. A stuffed bird of paradise adorned every head, and cheeks and shoulders were stained red. Flowers and leaves sprung from their calves and forearms. Necklaces jangled on naked chests. They were magnificent.

When we reached the broadest flat in the ridge on which the village perched the dancers fell into lines. The kundu drum of the old man beat rhythms that set the men flying. Low to the ground they danced, with bended knees and Cossack kicks, round and up and down. The old man would bark a word or two and start to chant and little dramas would be danced out. One told the story of the people's trip from the coast to the mountain ridge, another of a man who rescued his dog from drowning by diving under the waves for him. It was narrative, evocative, athletic and dazzling. The dancers worked like clockwork. It was so well drilled there was obviously one hell of a dance master at work behind the scenes. It was the best singsing I had ever seen.

As we shook hands with the elders before heading down the ridge I nodded towards the dancers. They were still dancing, sweating, working into a trance.

'Your dancers must do well at the cultural festivals with that singsing,' I observed.

'Would we?' replied one of the elders. 'We have never taken it outside of our village.'

The same party of porters and guides escorted us down the mountainside but this time the shyness had gone. We were all friends now. As we walked back along the switchback track Simon, Lynn and I discussed the dance. Simon had never seen anything like this Salemben dance and was very excited. Most of the coastal people had lost their vigorous singsing forms. Long years of missionaries had dissuaded them from dances of a powerful or sensuous nature. Even animal dances were labelled the work of the devil. Generally only the innocuous circle dances have survived. We had witnessed an important dance. Lynn had been a professional dancer and she was as impressed as Simon was. We couldn't work out how such a dance could be so slick and well crafted if they only did it for local events. Did they dance a lot just for their own pleasure? Was it a sacred dance that needed constant work in order to please the garden gods or somesuch? Moyang simply said that they always danced it like that. We pondered on the mystery.

On the long slippery hike back to the car we again walked bare foot. A frogmouth owl glided above our heads and a long arm snaked up and plucked it from the winds. We were offered the ugly, grumpy bundle of grey feathers as a pet. When we declined it was tossed gently back into the air. It unfurled into sharp wings of splayed feathers that punched the bird rapidly towards a tree. Above our upturned faces it seemed to slap into a trunk and stick as if by magnet. It glared dolefully at its former captors.

Another carrier, Yuk, saw a cuscus. He pointed it out to us; a tiny grey camouflaged ball wedged into a fork in a tree. Suddenly one of the young hunters burst into a run. He threw a heavy stick and knocked the frightened creature onto the floor. He chased through ferns and thickets and caught the lovely thing. The cuscus is a beautiful marsupial with a gentle face and featherboa tail. This one was not badly hurt, just scared and shaken. The little darling was also offered to us as a pet. The kids adored it, but we had a thing about wild things living in cages and declined pet number two. We watched the hunter free it.

Well, that's what we thought he was going to do, but instead of lifting it up to a branch he swung it around his head and bashed its brains on the path. It screamed with pain and fear. He swung again, and again, until it finally lay quiet. He smacked his lips. Lunch. As we walked down the track to the house below the ridge the kids kept looking at the bundle of fur as it swung from his waistband dripping blood.

While we rested and waited for a cup of tea I played Doctor Phil, cleaning and bandaging the suppurating sores of some local children. The smell of cooking cuscus filled the room. We declined to eat.

After that the track became rocky in places, and our feet bruised as we stumbled down the mountain. Moyang wished to know if his village pleased us and if it had tourism potential. Certainly it did. The principal attraction was not so much the rugged mountains or magic forests or sacred cliffs, it was the community itself. Spending a few days amongst these physically beautiful people, seeing their intricate dances and wandering through their gardens and their lives was a rare experience. We were enriched by the spiritual strength and cultural pride, and the simple kindness which kept us well fed, washed and safe on the slippery slopes. I sensed there was a market.

Back in Madang, Moyang and I talked in detail. It is a tricky problem to develop a sustainable tourism project. A stream of visitors destroys what they come to see. Resentment builds within a village if only a few people make money from the visits. Being on display can become tiring and demeaning. Our plan was to keep visits to less than fifteen trips a year, and to charge decent money for the experience. Other trek organisations paid villages a pittance for overnight trek stays and then wondered why the quality of the hosting rapidly deteriorated. We drew up payment schedules so that whilst the individual carriers, guides, cooks, dancers and cleaners would receive cash for their work a percentage also went into a community fund so that everybody would benefit. Moyang took the plans home and came back a few weeks later. The elders had given it the go ahead. I started looking for people to send, but my feelings were mixed. I was still concerned that I was passing over a poisoned chalice, and that the wonder of Salemben might be destroyed once opened to the world, though I knew it had all been dreamed and it was what the people wanted.

I organised a number of paying trips. Without fail the travellers I sent north made the effort to come to my office afterwards to thank me for my urging them on and up the mountain. The people of Salemben appeared to be perfect hosts. They were flexible and generous and gave each visitor the opportunity to explore their own interests. An elderly Australian woman who struggled up the ridge just wanted to sit in the gardens with the women. Throughout her travels in PNG she had seen only the displays of men and had no opportunity to observe women's culture. The women of Salemben did not let her sit quietly. They had her harvesting ripe vegetables and taro, and planting new seeds. They taught her all the stages of making a string billum bag — stripping the leaves, washing and dyeing, rolling the string on thighs and tying the knots. They told stories and giggled like sisters.

A strong young Australian male hunted the forests with bow and arrow one day and descended to the river valley to spear fish the next. A young boy overcame his fear of black people by playing spinning tops with village children.

One day a jaded English traveller loitered around the museum. He read the story of the Keki Lodge on the noticeboard and was a little cynical about the claims of a real Niugini experience. I quizzed him, and he told me that he had dreamed of visiting PNG since he was a child but had spent two months vainly trying to experience genuine cultural expression. He complained of singsing choreographed for westerners, fat dancers and bored guides. He had a week left before he went home. I convinced him to splurge the last of his kina and head up the North Coast Road.

He returned ecstatic. It was only then that he revealed to me that he was a professional dancer. In Salemben they discovered his trade. All afternoon they taught him singsing steps. That night everybody went to bed very early, and despite his excited energy he too managed to sleep. He was woken by painted faces and the lizard beat of Kundu. He was swept from his bed and dressed in full bilas, they painted his face and wove a bird through his hair.

All night they danced the dances they had taught him, for him, with him. He danced for hours and when he flopped in exhaustion they spun new dances to entertain. When he regained his breath they pulled him up to a familiar kundu beat and off he danced again. He found the PNG he had longed for.

Throughout my stay in Madang, Keki Trek and Lodge slowly blossomed. By all reports the community was happy with arrangements and slowly word began to spread amongst travellers and expats. The New Zealand government funded brochures to be printed. As the potential grew, I was still nervous about it, despite the dreaming. Had I helped save a rainforest or blemished the pearl?

I was asked to advise on another possible guesthouse.

Again the family travelled, this time to Manum Island, the perfect volcanic peak we had seen thrusting from the ocean to the west of Salemben. A lodge was planned for vacant land overlooking the reef and a spring water grotto on the beach. The women of the island would balance three bowls of water upon their heads, the biggest on the top, and walk with grace up steep inclines to their village. There were treks to the crater that still steamed from violent eruptions earlier in the year. The culture, with its intricate system of government by elders, is unique in PNG. The children were innocent and open, and ran naked without shame. I was torn again. I heard of no dreaming in this place to indicate that the visitors will be benign and paradise would absorb the disruption. There was a much bigger surrounding population than at Salemben, and I could envisage much jealousy from neighbouring villages.

On our way back from the island the outboard motor of our aluminium dinghy, the best boat the village owned, spluttered to a halt. We were halfway between the mainland and the island. It was a stunning place to be — volcano to the north, mountain ranges to the south — but a horrible place to wallow. I took stock while our hosts played with the engine and tried not to look worried. We were drifting in a strong current that ran between the island and the mainland. Past Manum the current poured north into the Pacific. It was only six hundred miles to the deepest ocean trench in the world. I didn't want to visit it. The boat flapped from side to side as the sun burnt down. Nina began to vomit. We drifted.

Someone on the roof of a ferry coming out from the island spotted us and soon hands were reaching down in rescue. A large woman held out her arms for Nina, who seemed to fold into her bosom and melt. She was nursed with total love. On the roof Ren and I were treated to risque jokes and a singalong.

When I realised how close to death we might have been I also realised that I had no right to question these people's desire to run lodges. It wasn't all paradise out here. In the wet it can be miserable, during eruptions terrifying — and the ocean is always dangerous. So if a lodge can raise money to buy a safer boat who was I to judge? Who was I to suggest that their culture should stand still? Change is inevitable. My job was to help advise them past the obvious pitfalls of an often callous industry. The choice was up to them.

I had no moral dilemmas with Malabo Theatre. They proved a hit with everyone. It was time to create a new work and the ensemble disappeared into their rehearsal loft for a week. Then Simon came to see me. They were stuck. There were too many ideas and nothing that inspired them all.

I thought for a few moments and said, 'Make me a play called *Keep Your Culture Strong*.' He smiled and disappeared again. The play they made, and performed in three languages, told the story of a rascal teenager in town who commits crime and is sent home to his father's village to learn respect and to be initiated. It became a big hit around the country, and was also loved by tourists. A play about contemporary problems and traditional solutions was a revelation to everyone.

One night Malabo travelled north to a dive resort for a special show. On their return Simon was very angry with me.

'You should have told me, should have warned us.'

'About what? What happened?'

'They were all Japanese. Everybody watching was Japanese.'

'I didn't know. I'm sorry.'

Simon had a problem with the Japanese. He could cope with individuals but as a group they made his blood run cold. During the World War Two, an American bomber had been brought down in the waters off Madang. Three airmen made it to Pig Island, where two were found and beheaded by the Japanese. The third hid under a reef, and was rescued by men from Simon's village. They hid him in the jungle and fed him for months. But one of the villagers was a Judas. To curry favour with the new masta he told the whereabouts of the airman. The Japanese caught him, kneeled him down in the mud and hacked the head from his neck. The men who had been hiding him, one of whom was Simon's grandfather, fled into the hills. To punish them the Japanese cut off Simon's grandmother's breasts. He couldn't forgive the race who did it, yet I've seen him entertain Japanese children with complete love.

We toured the play up into the Highlands and were just as successful there. For the performers it was confirmation of both their talent and the richness of the culture of Madang. In a country where cultural pursuits are as important as sport, the chance to represent one's province is regarded as a great honour. One night we performed all of the company's work at the spectacular Raun Raun Theatre. We attracted a large audience, many of whom were of Madang origins. When the initiation trumpets were sounded in *Keep Your Culture Strong*, many men in the audience shed tears of recognition and homesickness.

As we were in Goroka I took Malabo to Massi village to formally meet Launi, his village theatre company, and all my wantoks. Half of the ensemble were scared stiff and refused to go. I had to push them into the bus with words of shame. All their lives these coastal people had been told horror stories about ruthless, aggressive Highlanders. As I drove them to the village two young girls were shivering in fear.

We were honoured by ceremonial mumu (a feast baked in the earth) and welcomed with fine speeches from the elders. It was my task to respond, and despite the fears I managed a speech in Pidgin English. I introduced the troupe, explained where they came from and thanked my Massi relatives. It was rough as guts but did the trick. The mumus were opened and succulent steam flowed out of the earth and we feasted. Much later I had great difficulty dragging my young dancers out of Massi. They sat in roundhouses and made friends. Generations of xenophobia had been swept aside in an evening.

Simon had previously worked for Raun Raun Theatre, and had no fear of the Highlanders. Neither had Samual. Several months before our Highland trip Samual had come to my office and asked for a grant to buy a tape recorder. He had been a music student at the University of PNG, but had a bad year. His girlfriend, a Highlander, became very sick. In desperation he took her home to his mother's village outside of Madang to get her nursed back to health. His uncles refused the request. She was a Highlander and if she should die in their village her people would arrive demanding huge compensation. Samual begged them to save his loved one. They took her in. She died. Her people arrived. A convoy of four-wheel drive trucks and battered buses pulled up, threats were delivered and a demand made which would bankrupt the village.

Samual, who had returned to Port Moresby to finish his studies, heard about the threats and the blackmail. He flew to Mount Hagen and hitched up mountain roads and walked down tracks until he reached the village of his girl. He walked into the centre and announced his presence.

'It was me who begged my people to nurse your daughter. It was my fault. They cannot afford your demands and I cannot let you attack them. You call for payback. Take my life for hers.' Samual bared his chest and anticipated a spear. Instead his girlfriend's father embraced him.

'You are not our enemy, you are our son. Your bravery and love for our daughter has paid the debt. You are welcome in this village always.'

After all that Samual still had to return to Moresby and sit exams. His playing was excellent but he failed Psychology of Music and another academic unit, and was tossed out of uni. His teachers liked him, recognised his talent and wanted him to complete his degree. But he had to repeat the year, and had to sit out for at least twelve months. The staff encouraged him to take up a personal research project during that year to help persuade the academic council that he was worthy of a second chance. That was why he needed a tape recorder. He wanted to record the traditional music of the Rai Coast, the home of his father.

I couldn't offer a grant. The organisation was constantly on the verge of bankruptcy and I had instigated a policy that gave me no power to give discretionary grants. If the people knew I gave out money I would have been besieged. I had to say no to Samual. When he left the room I asked Simon's opinion. Like me he was impressed. I had a sudden thought to employ Samual as a musical director for Malabo and Simon agreed. We called Samual back and offered him a job. After a three-month trial he would become the musical director of the Provincial Theatre Company. He was flabbergasted. It was like a dream.

'You mean I get a weekly wage?'

'As of Monday.'

He almost wept. Later I discovered that his father had not been upset at his son's demise at university. It meant that the smart son with the big ideas could now stay at home and help run the family business — a chicken farm. Instead of a life of feeding, cleaning and slaughter he had another chance at music. He said we saved his life. I'm glad. He is a great musical director. He taught our women to beat the garamut drums (another taboo broken) which allowed all the men to dance together. He discovered how to play the ancient trumpets held in the museum. He trained our singers, and learnt to dance and act himself. He would have been wasted on the chickens.

Launi brought his company down to Madang to complete the exchange visits. Some of his performers had never seen the ocean. They were desperate for a swim, but a little unsure of the vastness of it all.

'Its quite safe down by the beach,' I assured them. 'The only thing to watch for are the black spiky sea urchins. Don't stand on them. Keep an eye out as they really hurt.'

Within five minutes the ensemble returned carrying the biggest of the warriors. He had stood on an urchin. His face was distorted with pain and the effort to control it. I had learnt the appropriate first aid when studying for my scuba ticket, but phoned the friend who trained me to be sure I had it right. I had. I gave my agonised wantok the bad news.

'First I have to crush the spikes within your foot, to break them into powder.'

'Do it then,' he grimaced.

'And to make the pain go away someone needs to piss on your foot.'

The company looked at me as if I had gone mad, but it

was true. The uric acid would neutralise the alkaline sting. Nobody volunteered, so I took on the job. I massaged the poor bastard's foot and felt the limestone-like spikes crumble beneath my fingers. He forced himself to remain silent but the pain was obvious.

'Do you want to get rid of the pain?' I asked.

He nodded and with wide eyes watched me undo my fly and piss on his foot. The relief was instant. It was a bizarre moment, the whitefella pissing on the warrior's foot, and we laughed like crazy.

Launi sent his company home, but stayed with us for a few days. He had to write a report to acquit his funding, and my computer and experience seemed valuable tools. That is why I sat one hot and humid night in my office pouring with sweat and slapping away mosquitoes as I hammered away on a keyboard. Launi had gone outside into the museum compound, leaving me to try to make sense of his handwriting. The sweat was rolling down my back and I began to get angry. When I couldn't read several scribbled notes I called out to him. There was no response. I soldiered on, until stuck again. Enough!

'Launi!' I shouted 'Launi, come and help me. Where the hell are you? Launi!'

There was a strange muffled call from a distance, then a long silence until his voice got closer. Eventually he came in the door. When he entered, dishevelled and confused, he looked awful. I stopped typing and asked what was wrong.

'I don't know. Something bad must have happened. Something made me go outside. Then I went crazy. I threw my watch away, up onto the roof, and my wallet into the bushes. I tore off my clothes, all of them. When you shouted for me I was already out of the compound, out on the road. Stark naked, true God. If you had not called me I would be out there still, wandering confused and naked until a policeman found me and beat me up. They do not like naked Highlanders down here. Thank you Wantok.'

He shivered and shook his head and looked frightened. I turned off the computer, we found the watch and wallet and I took him home. We had not been there more than ten minutes when the phone rang. It was his sister in Goroka. Poppa Doiki had passed away. The great old magic man was dead and, in his passing, had sent his son a little mad, had made him strip away his western veneer of clothes and clocks and money and sent him naked into the night. Or so it seemed.

Launi went home and I got back to work. There were tensions and problems to sort out. Local landowners were in dispute with some dive resorts over reef ownership and rocks were thrown. I had to enter a village accompanied by a policeman with a shotgun, which I did not enjoy. The local customs officer became jealous of my car and wanted to impound it unless we paid tens of thousands of dollars of duty.

I was continually having to fight for funds to be released so that I could pay my staff. I took to sitting outside the government offices on the day the cheques were due, sitting in the sun with the all the others who were promised money. I was the only whitefella and I stuck out like a sore thumb. The bosses were embarrassed by my waiting. 'Go back to work Phil. We will send the cheque.' I refused to leave without my workers' wages. It never took long for the cheque to arrive.

But the constant money troubles and petty rules, humidity, jealousy and stress began to wear me down. The kids got thinner and sadder as a variety of tropical bacteria discovered their succulent bodies and kept them sick. It had been eighteen months and it was time to find a successor and go home.

I visited Port Moresby to head hunt and attend a theatre conference. When I returned Lynn picked me up from the airport, and we drove home and parked the car under the house. It was a sad evening because I had a call from Goroka looking for Launi who had been in Moresby with me. His mother, Momma, had died. I spent a couple of hours trying to find him by phone, and then we went to bed early. We slept unusually late for the tropics where the early morning is a time to be treasured. We were packing for a picnic and I sent Nina downstairs to put something in the car. She immediately returned.

'Where's the car Dad?'

'Under the house.'

'No it's not.'

It seemed impossible that my beautiful car had been stolen. The house was surrounded by an eight-foot fence. Many wraps of a noisy chain, which awoke me with the slightest chink, secured the double gate. The dog was a coward, and went noisily berserk when anyone came near, but that night we all slept the sleep of the innocents. The house was regularly checked by a security guard who wandered the grounds of the adjacent museum, but he too had fallen into deep sleep. The car was a heavy diesel wagon, hard to start without a key, and very hard to push silently through the mud. But gone it was.

Weeks of difficulties followed. Without a car a white family in town becomes trapped at night, unable to brave the streets like the locals. We were looked after by daylight, and friendly eyes guarded the house, but anyone, from anywhere, could be abroad at night. The insurance company would take months, and we were leaving in a few more weeks. Other methods were suggested. Several old men offered to use sorcery to find the car. It was tempting, but I got bad vibes and chickened out. It was reported to have been seen in the Highlands, and I invited the police to use my office phone to make enquiries as they had run out of money to make long distance calls. All to no avail. We survived on foot, with the help of friends, and by hitchhiking to school with the kids in the morning.

A week or so before we left the country Launi, came down to the coast to bid us farewell, and the beautiful Pauline disobeyed her lordship's commands and followed him with the new baby. We had a wonderful night together, talking and laughing. That was the night we heard the story of how the two of them became married.

A decade before, when Launi was director of a Sepik theatre company in Wewack, Pauline was one of the dancers. One morning he arrived at work to find she had not come in. As she was a very reliable worker he felt slightly alarmed by her absence. The alarm slowly built until he felt it was more than just worry; that something was wrong and he was picking up the bad feeling.

When Pauline failed to front up the next day he set off to her village. He arrived to find her unconscious and dying. Apparently she had been working in the garden when someone blew powdered bone onto her, and she immediately collapsed. Her family had been expecting a payback sorcery killing from their rivals, and she was of the correct lineage to receive the retribution. Her people just laid her out and grieved.

He told me that he found her thin and pale and barely breathing. He tried to force water and food into her mouth and to shout and slap her back into reality. He could not break into her coma.

'That night,' he told us, 'I watched the flesh on her face just fall from her bones. It was incredibly quick. She was turning into a skeleton before my eyes.'

In desperation he went outside and summoned his father. Poppa came. Don't ask me how or what cosmic phone exchange the son used, but somehow Poppa, still living and thriving three hundred miles across the massive mountains, heard Launi's cry for help. He came in an instant and surveyed the scene.

'The people who are doing this have taken the form of fireflies. Catch them and they will do your bidding,' Poppa instructed.

'You have to understand,' Launi explained, 'that they may have had the bodies of fireflies, but they were humans nevertheless. I spotted them, five of them, flashing on a broad leaf. Knowing them to be human I pretended not to see them, and walked back into the hut. I found an empty coffee jar, and walked back outside. I acted easy, walked past them as if going elsewhere. Then I turned suddenly and trapped them in the glass. Quickly I slipped on the lid. I left them there a few moments, and then unscrewed the jar. I whispered, 'Let her live and I'll let you go,' and then tightened the lid again. You see Phil, when you have taken on the body of another you cannot just get out of it whenever you wish. You have to ride out the spell until the end. If your new body dies, so do you.'

A few moments later there was a noise in the hut, a small grunt followed by a gasp. Launi was called back inside. Pauline had stirred. Her eyes fluttered open, very weak but alive. He wet her lips, and forced some water between them. Gradually her breathing strengthened, and later she asked for more water. By morning it was clear that she would live. The fireflies were freed.

The next morning Pauline's father gave her to Launi.

There was to be no bride price. 'She was dead, and you gave her life. Now she is your wife.'

And a beautiful and bounteous wife she is too. Plenty of kids and a great strength to her husband. A woman who can cope with the irritable old bastard, who laughs and fights for her husband's honour and keeps him out of trouble. A marriage made in heaven, but not the kind I was told about in Sunday school.

When the story finished it was late. Lynn and I marvelled at the magic, and remembered Poppa Doiki. Launi finally asked 'Have you still got the necklace?'

There was an awkward, awful silence.

'No,' I admitted. 'It was in the car. When it got stolen.'

'Oh no. Why didn't you tell me! If we'd known that we could have found the car. That necklace was very powerful. We would have got your car back!'

'That's not important. The necklace ...'

'Ah it's gone now. We are not supposed to own such things. They pass through our lives. Whoever stole the car is being made to pay, you can count on that. Wouldn't want to be in his shoes. When did you say it was stolen?'

'That weekend we were in Moresby. You know, the night Momma died.'

He let out all of his breath.

And that's when we heard the full story of the necklace.

Launi's father had a collection of magic objects from his coastal village. He was a man with great spiritual power, and Launi had seemed to be born with the same. That scared Momma. One morning, when Launi was four or five, he was sitting on the kitchen floor when he was suddenly lifted into the air by some invisible force. It threw him out of the house and into a bee's nest outside. After she had extracted the stings from her boy Momma flew with a wild fury into the ancient artefacts. She grabbed them all into her arms, raced them to the river and flung them into the water.

When Poppa returned he ignored her wailing and carefully walked the track. He found a few pieces, and the broken necklace, which he rethreaded and hid. Momma had always hated having the dead snake in her house, so when Launi was leaving for Australia Poppa gave it to him to take away.

It was supposed to look after him, but Launi hated it. I think it reminded him of the power and knowledge he thought would never be his. Whatever, it was bad for him. He didn't want it, but it had to stay in the family. So as soon as he named me his wantok, his brother, he passed it on. In ignorant bliss I loved it, and I think it loved me in return.

'So now you know,' grinned Launi in triumph, 'who really stole your car.' We sat quietly around the table trying to make sense of all that we had heard.

'Are you suggesting,' I asked, 'that Momma stole the car? She couldn't drive, she was scared of cars.'

He shrugged and looked at me, with a grin. 'What do you think Phil? That it was just coincidence?'

A staggering coincidence. The night Momma dies the one powerful object she hated, and wanted away from the family, is stolen. Perhaps in death she finally had the power to weave the necessary magic, to scatter sleepy dust and lead the rascals towards my car. In the end the necklace returned to the jungle, leaving me with a taste of objects of power. Frightening and compelling.

I found a successor for my job from Madang and we went home.

Gateway

The kids got healthy but, after surviving the trials of PNG, my marriage blew up in the security of home. We travelled so well together, but back home my faults drove Lynn wild.

Amid the distress of the break up I still found the inspiration to apply for grants. I was not quite finished with PNG (I doubt I ever will be). The ribbon still unravelled, the necklace of my life required more exotic beads. I returned there eighteen months later to write a play for Malabo with a literature grant. It was something we had always planned, a PNG-Australian epic. This time when I arrived in Madang there was no welcome. I wasn't too worried and caught a lift to a hotel where I met my old mate Tim, the best scuba teacher in PNG. He was surprised to see me. Now I was worried. Tim was on the board of the Madang Visitors and Cultural Bureau, my previous employers. He should have been aware I was coming.

'Aren't I expected? I'm supposed to be working with Malabo.'

'We just folded the company last week. We had a funding shortfall about equal to the cost of the company and have put them off. Sorry.'

All that work down the drain. All the training and writing and rehearsal to create works which had now ceased to exist. I felt like crying, but changed the subject.

'Have you seen Simon? I'm supposed to stay at the new lodge in his village.'

'Simon left a couple of weeks ago. Got a job in Port Moresby.'

I was flattened. The company I had come to work with gone. My cultural adviser gone.

'So what are you doing Tuesday?' Tim asked.

'I don't know what I'm doing any day anymore.'

'Good. You can come on a dive trip up to Hansa Bay for a week. There is talk of a newly discovered wreck I want to try and find.'

There was no point lying around Madang feeling sorry for myself. I grabbed a couple of research books and left a message for the ex-Malabo performers that I had returned and would like to do a few days work when I got back. Tim and I trawled all night and day up the north coast and had wonderful diving for days. I read the diaries of the first white man in the area, Nikolai Mikloucho-Maclay, and a well-written text on the local cargo cults. I got fit carrying tanks when Tim fell ill with malaria. Perhaps I had the raptures of the deep, because one afternoon … the clouds began to tell stories.

As we cut through surging green waves towards a smoking volcano, I saw the heads of old men gliding across the sea. Invisible wind blew up the violently vertical slopes of Manum, gaining smoky form as it rose higher into cooler climes. Clouds grew on a massive scale, not just piles of friendly fluff but tangible shapes of noses, chins and eyes. A string of busts of ancient men streamed across Hana Bay and into the mountains on the mainland. Some looked up into the sun, and others back to the jagged peak and lava flows they left behind

I lay back against the wheelhouse and wondered who they were, and where they went, and why. Wished them well.

And then I looked to other clouds, beneath the heads — and saw one shaped like Malabo, a flying fox, his mousy head so clear I froze in recognition. He surfed our blustery headwind, wings stretched out to either side. As I watched this vapour beast its eyes took shape, took life, and swivelled in its head. It fixed me in its glare. I laughed and watched it vanish into tumbling whiteness.

Malabo is an important spirit on the Madang coast and I began to wonder if it *was* just a cloud that I had witnessed. I willed him back, and looked again — and there he was. So sharp this time, against the other floss. And battling hard it seemed, something pulling him, or pushing, towards the coastal plain. Again he looked at me; again he faded into background sky.

The apparition had been so vivid I was slightly stunned. Then I laughed again. The sun, sea air and tiredness, the wonder of the vista, were having their effect. I was seeing things, delightful things. I looked around for other shapes.

And saw two old men floating low towards the hills.

Pinch time. Is this for real, am I dreaming, am I stoned? Does it matter? Look more! Look more!!

Just clouds.

Drop it now. No! Look once more. The spray is in my face and I want more stories from the sky. I want these clouds to be more than vapour, and formulate a test. If I can see Malabo again I'll know this sky is special.

Nothing. No Malabo.

I call him then. 'Come Malabo. I promise I'll believe in

your existence if you'll come once more.'

And come once more he does. More distant now, less strong, but clear in his whiteness against the blue. Again his eyes glance towards me. They smile with confirmation, 'See. I'm here.' I nod back, bound by my word to believe. Then he turns again to his task at hand. There was some tension in it. He was battling — fighting? — No! He was getting out of the way.

Leaning back and opening wide my vision I now took in a whole new panorama. Between the mainland and the volcano, from the direction we were heading, blew a huge mass of air. Malabo had been surfing on its edges, but now was cast aside.

Way above, lining the roof of the sky, hung a huge flat cloud moving with the wind. Its head, high above mine, was like a drawing from my childhood books — a Chinese dragon, with trumpet nostrils. In awe I traced its serpentine body across the sky and discovered, high above its chest, yet another band of cloud. Lines of feathered wisps projected left and right forming jagged wings. And further back a tail.

Another laugh of pure delight spilt from my lips. This mirage was truly extraordinary — so huge, so clear. As it slowly sailed across the sky I felt it pulse with life.

Fear touched me, then bravado. I called up to it, 'I see you dragon. I know you are alive.' And baited it with dares to swoop on down towards me. Instead it ponderously turned its huge head until it fixed me with a glare. I suddenly feel a dreadful fear of this awesome thing. It stared with vile contempt, fixing me fast upon the deck, shrinking me. I am nothing in its eyes.

No, not nothing, for it bothers to look. It heard my call, and my human cheekiness niggles at its haughty power. I bother it, because I do not hang my head and hide. Pure malevolence beams at me from the sky. I freeze, and scarcely breathe.

The boat still ploughs through heavy seas. The dragon power is in my face, blowing hard. It pushes Malabo aside but not us. Slowly we make headway. Despite the elemental forces that surround us (the surging sea, smoking peak and dragon gale) we puny humans push on through. This knowledge makes me bolder.

Still the monster stares, neck lengthening as it twists its head towards me. I stare it down, stare back into the eyes of the chimera, and wish it bon voyage. Disdainfully it turns away and rides the winds northwest.

A dragon out of China, flying home. What brought it here, what changes does it predict? Will Malabo be pushed aside for good one day by the power of the dragon? How will PNG survive the Asian Tigers? I ask these questions of the clouds. Silently the sky dissolves its shapes, all except the two old men. They ponder as they drift.

I lay against the wheelhouse, spellbound. The things I had seen were real. The sky was a gateway that day and the winds had borne spirits. I was back in the land of magic and things were revealed to me again. Malabo had shown himself at my bidding and I was bound by my promise to believe.

This was the first time I had ever made a commitment of belief. I couldn't just shrug off this event as another quirky adventure. I had made a commitment to a pagan spirit. Malabo lives. The spirits still live. I breathed slowly, remembering a cave in Queensland. Remembering the night of lightning on Aramot when I believed in fairies again. I promised Malabo I wouldn't forget him.

Back in Madang the company had gathered, without a

claim for payment, to improvise with me for several days. I felt loved again. Then I headed north to revisit Salemben. I had exchanged regular letters with Moyang but wanted to see for myself how tourism had treated the village.

The small track that led off the North Coast Road had been broadened for the timber trucks to take their giant loads to the sea. The mud and sapblood formed quagmires. My heart bled at the destruction I saw. Thankfully before we reached Salemben the forest rape was over. They had not reached that high and Salemben is still safe above the clouds.

I walked in to a warm welcome. The next day I revisited the Cliffs of Henespe. Before we left the track to enter the sacred ground I asked Moyang to light a fire. Despite the wetness of the season he soon maked flames from dry fibres he found deep within a trunk. Meanwhile, I crush some West Australian bush incense. I let the red powder drop onto the coals and as the sweet white smoke snaked up into the jungle canopy I silently asked the spirits to accept my presence, and promised to respect the place. A bird instantly rose screaming from a branch above me and flew directly towards the cliffs, calling raucously as it went.

'Did you hear the bird?' asked Moyang.

'I certainly did.'

'Did you understand what it said?'

'No,' I laughed.

'It said it heard your thoughts and you are welcome. It has gone to let the spirits know that you are coming.'

This time the walk around the cliffs was silent and the rocks seemed more awesome. Without all the men and boys of the village tramping noisily, the place had the feel of a cathedral. A strange light, filtered through huge leaves and refracted off a thousand rivulets, created a sort of sparkling gloom. The birds were very attentive of our movement and everywhere hung the archaic smell of mushrooms. It was obviously a sacred place.

I was pleased to find no evidence of tracks. Moyang assured me that each group of visitors entered by different routes to ensure there was no damage. He said that business was a bit slack at times, but visitors kept coming. They had found a new market in city born Papuans who had never had a taste of village life. I thought that a healthy development.

The next day there was a special performance for me of my favourite singsing. I was invited to video the preparations which lasted for several hours. Costumes were laid out and mended, make-up applied. Bodies warmed-up and routines practised. The final adjustments were made and the finest decorations set in place. Then the dance master brought his dancers to focus. He slapped them and spat ginger in their faces. He kicked them behind the knees and placed pig tusks in their teeth. He started pounding on his kundu and the performance began.

He called the stories in a different order to the rehearsal. The men danced with vigour for the better part of an hour. Towards the end they were allowed to break ranks and slip into ecstatic dancing. Several managed the transformation into something other and writhed upon the ground until brought back to reality. They seemed to enjoy the experience of falling into trance.

I was told that because of my belief on my first visit that they would have success in the cultural festivals, the community had raised the money to take the group to Mount Hagen. It required three days of solid driving into foreign mountain country, but it was the country's top cultural festival, held only every two years. The Keki dancers won the prize for the best dance group in PNG. I felt jubilant. I also discovered the true provenance of the dance and why it had been so slick when my family had first seen it. When the old men had dreamt the Keki Dreaming, each member of the community had taken responsibility to do the right thing by the gods. The dance master knew that visitors would want to see singsing, so he set about forming a dance company. He remembered the dance from his youth and, now that there was a reason, he set about making it alive again. The costumes were designed, the steps choreographed, the bodies trained and strengthened. That first performance we had seen was in fact the world premiere. No wonder it was so tight.

Although the dance had been resurrected for travellers, it brought immense pride to the dancers themselves. For twenty years the young people had shown no interest in the old steps and now they lived again. I stopped worrying about Salemben.

Before returning to Australia I returned to Massi village to see my Niuginian family again. I spent a day or two working in the gardens and helping to make huge fires of the weeds and grasses we pulled. Fire lighting is a major part of Highland agriculture. Burning hillsides are a common sight. I'm not sure if it is ecologically sound, but it is a lot of fun, and a great reward for a hard day's work. Coming from a country where wildfire is so dangerous I am always nervously excited by a big burn.

The family was fit and happy. Except for Launi. He was very fit, but not happy. He insisted I visit Poppa's grave, but then told me not to open my door at night in case his spirit came walking. He professed to be very angry at his father. He could not understand how Poppa could have departed without instructing him in his magic arts. To have a father who could fly his spirit across the world to help his family, then passed on without handing on the secret knowledge was very hard to take. Launi wanted to be able to offer his own children the protection his father had given him, but the gateway was closed. The family magic was seemingly at an end and Launi still grieved the loss.

One evening he approached me, agitated, to ask a favour. He wanted me to forbid my young nephew Dillon from walking alone on the hillside behind the gardens. I was puzzled. Why would the authoritative Launi need me to tell his son anything, and why would he want to ban his son from enjoying the pleasures of a beautiful hill?

'Why don't you forbid him yourself?' I inquired.

'I have told him not to go many times. He does not listen. If he comes home from school and no one is here waiting at the house, he wanders across the creek instead of doing his work. I fear he goes up the hill. He loves you, Phil, and respects you. If you tell him not to go I think he may listen.'

'I don't understand your concern. He's just acting like any young boy, running away from work. I would be pleased if my kids wanted to play out in the sunshine and fresh air. What's the problem? The hillside is beautiful.'

'What if he were to get hurt when he was alone up there?' Launi threw back. 'He could be lying alone in the darkness and we would not know where to find him.'

'Yes, that's a possibility, and every parent's fear. But do you want to stop him going anywhere alone, do you want to hold him to your garden forever and not see the world?'

'No.'

'Do you mind him going on the other side of the village?'

'No, it is only that hill where he must not wander. Please wantok, he will listen to his uncle.'

'Why mustn't he go there? I can't forbid him something I cannot understand.'

'You mustn't tell him, but there is a … how do I put this? … a gateway, you know, a gateway there to … to the otherside. You know what I mean. A place where a young boy with powers like he has might be endangered. We might lose him. Please help.'

I suddenly realised the problem. My nephew, like his father and grandfather before him, had been born with power. Just as Launi had been too young to handle things, his parents now worried that Dillon was also too young to handle such power. He had the frightening ability to freeze his older sister into mute stillness if she ordered him around once too often. His parents had to tell him to let her go. To me however he was just a normal, lovable kid, full of normal urges and desires. He was my mate, and followed me everywhere and had never given me a sign of any strange power or a propensity to be a spiritual bully. A bit cheeky, perhaps, but a great kid.

Now his father was begging me to pull his son back from a dangerous brink, back from the temptation of the otherworld. It was taking an enormous amount of face for Launi to ask this, to admit that he was unsure how to raise this difficult child. Yet it was in a sense almost ludicrous, to ask a whitefella to warn a Niuginian about the spirit world, to expect that I had an answer to his son's possible attraction to a magic realm to which I had no access. My head spun with responsibility and incredulousness. I almost laughed, but it wasn't funny.

'Please Phil.'

'I can't,' I finally answered. 'Or rather I don't think I should. He might well listen to me while I am here, but soon I will be gone. I can't explain it to him properly because I don't understand. And I fear that if I warn him it might just interest him more to visit once I have left.'

'Then I don't know what to do.'

'Have you been over there with him? Do you know that he is attracted to this "gateway"?'

'No.'

'Well I think you must, brother. One thing I do know about kids is that they will do the opposite of what they are told if it seems exciting and they do not understand the consequences. Just warning him not to go, without saying why, will just send him over determined to look for the danger. Go walking with him over there. Father and son. See if he's attracted to the dark place. If he's not, then you can sleep easy. If he is then you can sit with him and scare him shitless about the spirit world.'

Launi clicked his tongue, nodded his head negatively and walked away. 'I thought you would help,' he muttered as he walked off into the dark. I lay disturbed for most of the night afraid, I had let him down. I thought perhaps I would do as he asked, but was unsure how to go about it.

The next day he returned to me. 'You are right, brother. It is my duty, not yours. I will go walking with my son. Thank you for your advice.'

I have been very lucky to wander with friends through a country where the spirits still roam strong, where garden gods are still evoked and ancient rituals call magic beings into existence. With the pride and security of owning their own land and being in control of their own destiny, the cultures of PNG still thrive. The magic plays upon the clouds and in open village squares to be witnessed by whoever passes through.

By travelling with locals, and in giving small gifts of performance and first aid as I pass, I have been rewarded with great gifts of remarkable happenings. It is as if the spirits of the place have sized me up and told me, like they did my son, 'You're all right boy, don't worry,' and not worrying themselves, have flaunted their existence in my face.

When I first visited PNG I was an unbeliever. A scientist of sorts. I am changed.

Blackfellas

In my home country of Australia the world's most ancient cultures still hang on to life, but have been so battered and dislocated by the white invasion that their practices are utterly secret and the power well hidden. The ancient knowledge and magic is not for me to know, but it influences anyone who lives upon the land. There lies another ribbon of experience that has moulded my being and opened my eyes.

Back in the early seventies, when I was at university, I started to develop a humanist political outlook, and began a lifelong interest in the struggle of Aboriginal people. In those days I had no inkling of the wonders of indigenous culture and spirituality. This was pure political and social concern. I was studying law, and the State Law Society decided to survey the needs and situation of the Nyoongars (Aboriginal people of the south-west of Western Australia). They called for volunteers and I found myself, with a former draft resister friend of mine, in the south-western wheat belt.

There we were, with our long hair, army jackets and badges, in cowboy territory. We naively wandered through a small town asking the questions on our list. The answers we got were not pleasant, and it took about five minutes for the town to know our business and reject us. We were refused food in a cafe, then chucked out of the pub. Finally a policeman forcefully suggested we move on. We drove out to the Nyoongar reserve bruised and looking for comrades.

We found a block of land fenced with wire and filled with derelict housing and scrap-built humpies. It was a couple of miles from town. Just close enough to ensure the kids who had to walk to school did not qualify for a free bus service, but far enough away to be out of sight. It was next to the town rubbish tip and stank. There was only one tap for a hundred people and the toilets didn't work. We were appalled, but perhaps even more upsetting was that these people were just as unwelcoming as the white townsfolk. They didn't see us as partners in their fight for justice, just as more meddling white folk pretending we had their interests at heart. The women were ragged and shy, the kids snotty and fly blown, the men aggressively dismissive.

We drove our Volkswagen back to Perth in silence and defeat. I saw at last how isolated we were in the beautiful gardens of academia. University had been good for me, but I couldn't be happy with its escapism any more. It was time to leave and see the world.

My first real Aboriginal friend was Paul Pryor. Like Launi I met him at drama school and like Launi he led me on bizarre adventures. This was the same Paul I had sat with in Popeye PK's healing pool. He was the most open blackfella I had ever met, free with his stories and his ideas. He told of running away from home in Townsville as a young teenager and heading bush. He made his way through to the Territory and lived with old fellas for weeks at a time. It gave him a dreaming of sorts which his urban Catholic upbringing had denied him.

In Townsville, his home town, we arranged for a performance of *The Murri and the Martian* in the civic mall to entertain the late night shoppers. Hundreds turned up, about a third of whom were blackfellas. It was a strange audience mix for the redneck town, but they all settled into the amphitheatre with their bags of shopping at their feet.

Early in the play Paul's character, a runaway kid, stands by a river and laments the blood of his people spilt in the calm waters. It was a poem Paul had written as a child, and thus quite apt, but the white Townsville crowd was maddened. They weren't having their kids affected by poetic politics of horror and they started to leave. Bags were pulled together and children grasped. A great heaving movement began, as in an ant's nest you have just stood on. But before the angry crowd could leave, the next scene began. Cute animal characters danced onto stage and sang a bush welcome. The kids demanded to stay; the parents relented and sat back down with their bags clutched tightly to their chests.

For half an hour the leave or stay tension bubbled. When the story got too political (a trip to a uranium mine, tourists on the sacred rock of Uluru) the white parents tried to move their charges, but the comedy and music won them back. Slowly they accepted and relaxed. Then, towards the end of the performance, a very drunken Murri woman staggered down the aisle and up to the actors. Paul and the Martian were performing a scene in the audience and quickly fled back onto the stage. This didn't stop the woman, who threw her leg in the air, her dress over her head, and struggled up to join them.

'What you doing, having a fuckin' party without me? Let's party!'

The audience groaned in unison. The Murris and Islanders hung their heads in shame and the white folks glared knowingly. 'Here we go,' you could sense them thinking. 'You almost had us conned into believing this story of cultural understanding. The fantasy almost won us over. But here's the reality, the drunken ugly reality of mixed race living come to ruin your play like it ruins all our lives.'

Paul looked at the drunken woman and the expectant angry faces of the audience. He put his arm around the woman and, staying in character, asked her to join him. 'My mum and dad are waiting over home for me. You want to come and meet them?'

'Yeah, I'll meet your mum and dad.'

'Come on then, come home with me.'

'Yeah, I'll come home with you,' she happily replied, and together they waltzed off the stage. The audience responded with a standing ovation. Paul had rescued the moment magnificently by including the woman in his story. He treated her with respect and she responded accordingly. Here was a lesson for the white Queenslanders who watched, and they knew it. Their dangerous preconceptions of Aboriginal people had been turned upside down. Paul's leading role performance had demonstrated his creative intelligence and capacity for hard work, and his improvisation demonstrated his humanity. People's lives are changed by such experiences.

Three years later, when I was living in Albury-Wodonga directing a theatre company, I heard that Paul and his pregnant wife Juliet had been forced out of Townsville by the police. Apparently he had designed and performed on an award-winning float in the Townsville Festival parade. He was the first Murri to win the award and his large extended family turned up in force at the outdoor concert where he was to receive his prize. While Paul was waiting in the wings for his big moment a bunch of redneck whitefellas started to hassle his family who were spread out in a prime spot in front of the stage. The bully boys wanted them to move to the side where all the rest of the Murris were camped but Paul's mum refused. They had Paul's dinner waiting for him, and they had as much right to this piece of land as anyone else. Paul heard of the dispute and ran into the crowd just in time to hear his mother cop a mouthful of disgusting abuse. He demanded an apology and received a tirade himself. He stepped forward and a brawl began. Instantly a pack of uniformed police pounced and piled on top of him. Juliet jumped on top of the pile of blue and punched into the backs of the men who were beating her man.

It turned out that the original abuser of Paul's mum was an off duty policeman. Thus Paul was charged with assaulting a police officer, as was Juliet. But so many other whitefellas in the crowd stepped forward to help defend Paul that he got off. The magistrate concluded that as the abusive cop had not identified himself as a police officer the charge could not be sustained. Juliet, on the other hand, had no such excuse as the men she hit were in uniform. The fact that she was pregnant, full of strange hormones and witnessing her man getting the crap beaten out of him was apparently no excuse. She was heavily fined. On the way out of the court other officers pulled Paul aside. 'You have three days to get out of town you black bastard,' was the gist of the message, but the language was much worse. Ejected from his home town Paul and Juliet returned to Melbourne, refugees in their own nation.

I organised some work for Paul teaching dance to the local Aboriginal kids and he, Juliet and baby Likaya moved to Albury. The teenagers Paul worked with had also been removed from their country. They had been relocated with their families from the far west of New South Wales to this southern district and were as depressed as any lost peoples. Paul gave them hope and pride, but he was losing those qualities in himself as he did so. He was being eaten from the inside by the bitter realities of being black. This was the man who did one good deed every day, like the boy scouts, because he loved the confusion and the twists of understanding he created by helping white people. I remember him offer to carry a heavy bag for an old lady. She clearly feared he would steal it. By the time he'd carried it to her house she loved him. Now this generous man was drinking too much and wallowing in anger. When he hit Juliet, I lost patience with him. I told him that if he hit her again our friendship was over. We began shouting at each other. He yelled that I didn't understand. I agreed. Rather than disturb the neighbours we drove down to the river to have it out, to see what could be resolved and whether our friendship could be salvaged.

We sat beside the mighty Murray River, leaning on the red trunk of a huge river gum. The water flowed unceasingly towards a distant sea. I asked him what was consuming his soul, but he shrugged away my concerns and changed the subject. He asked me about the breathing cave, still wondering what it had meant. What was it about me, he wondered, that made me able to hear a cave breathe and sit comfortably with an angry Murri. 'What has made you accepting of other ways and comfortable with your black brothers?'

'I don't know. My brother John shares some of that, so

maybe it's a by-product of being a twin, or the genes we received from our gregarious father.'

'Do caves breathe for them?'

'I don't think so.'

'What changed you?' asked Paul.

'So that I can see red lights in villages and dragons in the sky? I don't know Paul. Does it matter?'

'Yes. If all the gubbas could be opened to the truth the destruction might stop. If others listened like you to the earth it wouldn't keep having the shit ripped out of it.'

'Bullshit Paul. You're aware of these things yourself, but you are still a destructive bastard.'

'We are not talking about me. I want to know what changed you.'

'What changed you Paul? Why all this anger and bitterness now?'

'I don't know brother. I'm fucked up inside. When I was a little boy I was sexually abused. Perhaps that is the cause of the pain.'

He cried a little and I hugged him.

'I'm a lost cause,' he murmured.

'Bullshit. You've just made two feature films. You have loving parents and a beautiful daughter. What the fuck is the problem with you?'

'I'm lost.'

'Paul, you have to get hold of yourself, you —'

'Don't yabba. Don't get me going. Don't get me angry. You're a mad bastard, sitting out here all alone with an angry Murri. I could beat the shit out of you.'

'Are you planning to?'

'No, but if you get started on me I might.'

'Bullshit.'

'How come you're happy to sit with a poor prick like me?'

I didn't know. I couldn't explain this strange attraction for indigenous culture. I liked the poor pricks. They gave me openings into other worlds that my gut told me was important. But they could be scary bastards.

I told Paul about coming back south, after the breathing cave, with sliced tendons in one foot. For some reason I forget, I was waiting for a friend at the Builders Arms, an infamous Koori pub in Melbourne. The Chairman of the Fitzroy Aboriginal Community wandered into the crowded bar and recognised me.

'Hey bro,' he greeted me in a friendly way. 'You're that bloke with that play, that play with the Kooris in it. That was you, hey?'

'That's me,' I smiled. It's always good to be recognised in a friendly way by the boss when you are in strange territory.

'The Fitzroy All Stars are holding this benefit night next month, for all the sports teams the kids play in. You should bring that play down, help us out.'

'We'd love to,' I explained. 'But both the Murris in the show have gone away. Paul, you know the bloke with the main part, well he's gone to Alice Springs to work with CAAMA radio. And Mick, the other Koori, he's up in Sydney with the Aboriginal and Islander Dance Company.'

'Well that's fucking typical that is.'

'What is?' I asked, starting to feel vulnerable.

'Gubbas like you. When it suits you to work with the poor blacks you're over us like a rash, but when we ask for help it's too much bloody trouble.'

'No, that's not what I said. We can't do the show even if we wanted to, it's finished now.'

'You could get it back together if you wanted to!'

'Paul is in Alice, Mick in Sydney. It would cost a thousand bucks to fly them back.'

'Just what I said. Typical fucking whitefella. Only willing to help when it fucking suits you.'

At that I saw red. Until then I think I had been a bit of a softie when it came to Aboriginal people. I understand the impulse of reverse racism. Most of the time blackfellas are not allowed to get away with anything, as you soon learn when you travel with them and find yourself meeting a lot of policemen. So you start to feel sorry for them and let them get away with things that you would not allow other people to get away with. But that morning, in the Builder's Arms, I had been abused once too often.

'You've no right to say that to me,' I burst out.

'I'll say what the fuck I want to. You're just like all the other white cunts.'

'Bullshit. I told you why we couldn't help.'

'Cos it's too much bloody trouble.'

'No!'

From there it just escalated. We were both yelling and cursing at each other. Finally he swung around and stormed out of the door and onto the street. I froze. What the hell did I think I was doing? I was yelling at the local community leader in a major Koori pub. It was packed, and I was the only whitefella. I felt suddenly small and scared.

A hand slapped me on the shoulder. I spun around on my one good foot expecting the worse. A big black face was grinning at me, a complete stranger.

'That was bloody great mate,' he bellowed. 'That bastard has needed a good talking at for some time.' The mob around the bar cheered and I was bought drinks all afternoon.

It's a matter of acceptance. Once I stood up for myself the people at the bar accepted me as a full human being. I was not some half-arsed, uncomfortable, out of place whitefella but a simple bloke who spoke his mind. Much easier to understand and much more fun to be with. And after that afternoon I found that I could more easily accept the fact that I had nothing to be ashamed of when it came to blackfella history. It's when I started to stand up for myself.

Paul laughed at the story, but he didn't stand up for himself. Behind the smiling eyes was a bitter deadness I didn't like. I stopped telling stories and looked at the water.

Paul went back home to Queensland. I encouraged it, believing his own land might nurture him. He phoned me at my office one morning.

'Hey Phil. I'm just going to the tree where my brother hanged himself. I'm going to do the same. I'm phoning to say goodbye.'

For an hour I cajoled and yelled and pleaded, tears on my face and panic in my heart. I begged him to think of his little girl, his parents, his students, the fight of his people. I told him I loved him. When he hung up I had no idea what he would do.

He was back in town a few weeks later, mad and drunk. He biffed his woman and came to me for help in getting access to his daughter. I threw him out and never saw him again. Six months later, after being arrested once again and having his face pushed in shit by the cops, he stopped the pain with a rope around his neck. I felt empty when I was told. I had no feelings about his departure. All the love and the hate I had for him was lost somewhere. I didn't grieve his passing. Not then.

A decade later, in Townsville on tour with *Bidenjarreb Pinjarra*, I visited Paul's mum and dad for the first time since he had taken his life. His mum, Dot, talked to me in a dark living room holding her emotions tightly clenched as we remembered Paul. Behind her hung an enlargement of the cover of the book *Maybe Tomorrow,* written by another son, Boorie. It is a photomontage of the three children Dot has lost to suicide, and the dead grandson who drove like a maniac in a stolen car. I was ineffably sad. Her husband Monty was in hospital getting a new knee. He was really pleased when I visited and we had a good chat. And a good cry. I went to find Paul's grave. They said it was difficult to find but I walked straight to it. I kicked the headstone, slapped it, and pounded it as I cursed and shouted at him. I wanted him to know the pain he'd left behind. I spat my anger, screamed my frustration, cried my love. I finally grieved.

That night we smoked the Civic Centre very thoroughly. Many indigenous cultures use smoking ceremonies to clear unwanted spirits, but that night I used ours to summon one. I walked behind the theatre calling on Paul to attend my performance. I sent my message out upon the wind, daring his shade to come into my light. It is well known that grief can send you mad, so maybe that is why I believed he was in the auditorium that night. Several of us sensed him in the dark at the back of the hall.

After Lynn and I had had enough of small town living in Albury-Wodonga we moved west to Perth with an eighteen-month-old Ren. I obtained a short-term job with the government and renewed my connection with Nyoongar theatre. The south-west peoples have a curious affinity to the theatre; it seems to suit their culture. Certainly West Australian Aboriginal theatre has been the most successful in the nation over twenty years. From the early seventies, Middar was touring the world with Ernie Dingo and Richard Walley. Then Uncle Jack Davis began to write his masterpieces such as *The Dreamers* and *No Sugar*. These encouraged Sally Morgan, and the Kimberley mob (Jimmy Chi's *Bran Nue Dae* and *Corrugation Road*) and the formation of Yirra Yaakin, a highly successful indigenous company. The theatre-going community has embraced black theatre and, unlike the situation in other parts of Australia, big mobs of blackfellas come to the shows. Theatre has raised Nyoongar pride substantially.

One day I heard that director Marcelle Schmitz had a wonderful project planned and I worked hard to be included. She had a dream, to take a team of Aboriginal and non-Aboriginal artists into the bush to work for a month to create a new play. She wanted to set us free from walls and roofs and conventional play making formulas. She wanted us to be able to live together as we worked, believing that this would breed a deeper understanding. She wanted to conjure a creation process that flowed through day to night without clocks and domestic concerns.

She chose multi-skilled actors who offered talents other than just the ability to slip into other skins. Some were fine musicians, some writers, artists, and some dancers. The ensemble was most impressive, and I got myself aboard. There were five blackfellas and six whitefellas, four women and six men.

Originally we were to travel north to station country, but the pastoralists who were to be our hosts let slip negative feelings about blackfellas and Marcelle decided to beat a hasty retreat. Instead we went south to a ghost timber camp in the bush. Usually used for school camps and the like we had the old township to ourselves, except for the crazy old couple who minded the place and a hermit who collected seeds from the bush. We were alone, surrounded by beauty. Kangaroos and emus wandered past the houses and kookaburras fought for our scraps. The nights were cold and clear with vivid stars, the days alive with crackling energy.

We did fantastic work, flying high with daring propositions and scraping close to the bone with brutal honesty. Tears, laughter, anger, exotic song and wild dance. We found a story and devised a script that I wrote down over thirty frantic, inspired hours in front of a computer in my sleep-out overlooking the bush. Together we made a brilliant play of epic proportions which will one day hit the stage and inspire the nation — as soon as one of us becomes powerful enough to raise the filthy lucre. It tells of a time in the near future when the ancient spirit beings again rise from the earth and discover an Australia utterly changed by the European invasion. Like a Greek epic it mixes gods and mortals and offers an inspired view of contemporary life. Look out for *Wel-le Dan-joo* at a theatre near you!

There was magic in that forest. With all the energy pumped out from a mob of wonderful people it is not surprising that the spirits of the place awoke and came calling.

On the third morning we left our huts before dawn and walked a couple of kilometres through the bush to an old dam. Steam rolled out of our mouths and burned slowly off the surface of the water as the sun rose through the ranks of dead tree trunks. Murray, one of the actors, led us through a ritual of embracing the environment and then into a personal, imaginary journey through our minds. It was a simple visualisation exercise in which he described a basic skeleton of a story upon which each of us created a unique fantasy adventure. Then we shared the stories, which were profound and funny and bizarre.

Then Murray asked, 'Did anyone else hear clapsticks?'

'Yes,' we all replied. During the exercise all of us had heard, quite distinctly cutting across the silence of the lake, three hammers of a pair of clapsticks. *Clack ... Clack ... Clack.*

We wondered if any bird made such a sound, but doubted it. Each was sure of clapsticks. *Clack ... Clack ... Clack.*

Then we discovered that half of us had heard them only a few minutes into the visualisation, the others towards the end. How bizarre. No one had heard them twice; each had heard them once. That set us into deep thinking.

Several mornings later I was conducting a movement class. Everyone was in a big circle, each moving with an object to the tempo of their own dance. I heard clapsticks again, far off to the right in the bush. *Clack ... Clack ... Clack.* Three of the company broke their movements and looked towards the sound, and then over to me. We smiled and kept our secret and carried on with the exercise.

A few days later we were working hard in small groups. My bunch had been caught up with the passion of our work and were late to get back to the meeting place. It was dark as Franklin and I walked up the track, and I was pleased to realise that we were not the last to arrive as I heard the music group just behind a fence, playing clapsticks. But when we entered the house everyone was waiting for us. No one had been playing outside in the dark. Frank and I shared that in secret too. *Clack ... Clack ... Clack.*

Then we had a visit from a local Nyoongar elder who

spent the day showing us how to make tools and weapons with traditional materials. He demonstrated a local bush incense and gave us a simple smoking ritual to use, which many of us have adopted. We asked him about the clapsticks. He smiled. 'So the sticks are here for you. That's a very good sign. It is the spirits of this place, the guardians, saying you are welcome. You are looked after here.'

They remained with us for the rest of our stay.

One night, towards the end of the month, there was a pool competition in town, forty minutes drive down the track, and our top players were anxious to beat the locals in the redneck timber town. The mood was for a party, we'd been isolated for three weeks and the crazies were stirring. Everyone was going, except me. I had to begin writing the next day and I knew it was going to be a very long stint in front of a computer screen. I needed to get a good night's sleep.

'Leave me,' I insisted, but they wanted me to come. 'I can't afford to get pissed, I need to keep my head clear,' but all that meant in their minds, was that I was the perfect driver for the expedition. I prevailed.

'You're a piker, Thomson,' they chortled as the bus pulled out and left me in peace. Beautiful, quiet, isolated peace. I was free of them. I went to bed.

I awoke in the dead of night, with the wind in my room. It swept around in circles, billowing the curtains and picking up the waste paper. A mini-tornado in my sleep-out, a personal willy-willy whishing round the room.

I sat up straight, wide awake, and watched in mute amazement as this invisible serpent of wind circled my bed, its course marked with litter and dust and the billowing curtain. Then it left, head first out the window, taking the curtain with it until the tail flicked and was gone. Leaving behind a message in my skull.

'*Beware the stranger!*'

Those three words were left ringing in my brain. Words I couldn't remember hearing, but they had got there somehow.

'*Beware the stranger!*'

I lay back in the darkened stillness. There was no more wind. The night was calm and black. Only the silent words remained. 'Beware the stranger.' I rationalised the experience eventually. It must have been a dream, both the wind and the message. What else could it have been? A dream, that's all. I settled back and tried to sleep, but argued against my conclusion. That was no dream — yes it was — bullshit — shut up and go to sleep —

'*Beware the stranger!*' Shut up!

A sound in the distance, a low, mosquito hum that slowly got louder. The bus returns. I followed its travels from the sounds it made, gear down for the turn off, accelerate again, break and stop, the squeaky wrench of gate, tyres spinning in the gravel to set off again, up the drive and then a final, sliding stop. Right outside my cottage. The one I share with Kelton Pell and Franklin Nannup.

'Not here, please,' I prayed. 'Don't get out here to party on, go to someone else's place. Please.' I heard the mob spill out and wander down the slope. Then Kelton spoke to someone.

'This is our place, and that's the other men's house next door. Next one isn't ours, but the third house up is the women's house, and then the family one.'

I froze. Kelton was explaining our set-up. He was obviously talking to a *stranger*. For three weeks we had lived alone. We had an unwritten law that we would hold our group solid for the month. One weekend partners and kids came down, but otherwise we kept things pure. Just us, no guests, no distractions. For the first time our solidarity had been breached, and I had just been warned. *'Beware the stranger'*.

I had never had prescience before. What did it mean, what should I do?

My sanctuary was breached as the fly door jerked open and the party entered the house. I tried to ignore it, but couldn't. I had to see this stranger and suss him out. I got dressed and went into the lounge. First thing I saw was him, the stranger. He sat directly across from the door and looked up to see me, a stranger in his eyes, enter the room in a troubled mood. I must have given him a very weird look; visibly he stiffened. We stared at one another.

'Hey bro,' greeted Kelton as he threw an arm around my shoulder. 'We're going to party on here for while, that all right by you?'

'Um, er no, not really,' I stammered, trying to get hold of things. 'We're starting early in the morning.'

'Says who?'

'Says all of us. We agreed at this morning's meeting, remember?'

'No.'

'Bullshit Kelton, you were there.' I was suddenly mad and angry, and taking it out on Kelton, which is not a good idea. I spun around and stormed out, slamming the door behind me. Kelton was instantly after me.

'Don't you fucking slam doors in my face!' and he was on me. Franklin followed rapidly and jumped between us.

'Hey, cool it you two. We're supposed to be working together, getting on.'

We stopped snarling and spitting and just glared.

'Come into my room and have a smoke,' ordered Frank, and we dutifully followed. We sat on Frank's bed, and I calmed down and realised how weirdly I'd been acting. I apologised to Kelton, and told my story of the wind in my room and the message in my head. 'Beware the stranger.'

Kelton and Franklin believed my tale instantly. Blackfellas, even urban ones, don't doubt the spirit world, they know it exists. They tiptoed over to the door and peered through the hinge crack to spy on the newcomer. I asked who he was. They didn't know. They weren't sure who had invited him onto the bus and home for the night. They thought that it might have been Ningali.

That might explain things. Ningali was the only one with the power to flout all group conventions and bring home a friend. She was raised traditionally and knew both worlds and obeyed what laws and lores she honoured and flouted all the rest.

So what was I to do? Tell the Queen to beware her consort? I asked my housemates for advice, but they just shrugged. I wandered out into the lounge, most uncertain and feeling strange. Ningali, of course, picked up my vibe and asked if I was okay. I said yes but she didn't believe me and called me over to where she stood. She wrapped long arms around me and asked me what was wrong. I couldn't say, because next to me the stranger sat, looking up and listening with intent.

'Hey Phil,' he said with false friendliness. 'You look buggered mate. We woke you up. Why don't you sit here, and I'll stand there.'

'I'll stand there —' what a line. He meant between those sinuous black arms. He was jealous, thinking Ningali and I might be lovers and that I was threatening his potential night of passion. Again I acted badly;

snarled, 'Keep your bloody chair,' and left the room. I kept on walking, out the back and up the slope into the blackness beyond. What a fool I felt. I was completely out of my depth, but I couldn't just go to bed. I knew I had to *'beware the stranger,'* but how? I got colder and colder staring at the vivid stars searching for an answer.

An answer came with Ningali coming out of the back door heading for the toilet. I reached the back verandah as she came out of the dunny and asked her for a chat. For the second time I told of wind and message. She grinned and squeezed my shoulder.

'So the wind is talking to you, that's a good sign bro,' she enthused, and thought deeply for a few seconds. 'Who is that bloke anyway?'

'I don't know. Kelton and Franklin thought you brought him onto the bus.'

'I don't know who he is. I thought the boys brought him.'

We both felt a little flick of fear. The mysterious man really was a stranger. Our warm and friendly mob had allowed him to infiltrate without questions. He could be anyone, he could do anything.

'You go and sleep in my room,' she decided. 'You need to sleep and we'll be keeping you awake.'

'It's all right,' I argued. 'I can just move next door and sleep in the other men's house.'

'No, you use my room,' she ordered. 'I never sleep in it anyway, I always sleep in front of the fire in our front room. So you use my bed, okay?'

'Okay.'

So I picked up my bedding, walked up the road and lay down in Ningali's bed. It seemed very strange, and I couldn't figure why I was there.

I awoke to a sparkling morning. I found Ningali asleep

in front of the fire, and was served breakfast by the other women, a much better feed than what was on offer at our place. When I got home I found out that the stranger had been given a mattress on the floor for the night before being driven out to the highway to hitch home first thing in the morning. He was gone.

We'll never know what threat he offered to our group. Perhaps it was just a coincidental dream that woke me up, but I don't think so. Neither did Ningali. She sent me to her room on purpose, perhaps to put a man in the woman's house in case he really was trouble. Not that I think those women needed any help at all, but if the wind bothers to call and warn there must be some sort of danger that needs serious consideration.

Coming out of Ningali's room that morning I glanced over to the house next door. That cottage had nothing to do with our gang; a quiet bloke who made his living collecting seeds from the forest owned it. He had been away on a gathering trip for a few days, and on his verandah I saw a cat.

A cat! This was a conservation zone, and domestic pets like cats and dogs were taboo. The seed gatherer was a forest lover; there was no way he would have a pet. I looked closely at the feral, but as I looked at the thing it shape-changed. Its nose shrank back into its face, and I sensed another body beneath. Not a curled feline shape, but something … manlike? I looked closer, in wonder, and poof! It disappeared.

I'll never know for sure, but I think I saw a widgardgee, the Nyoongar word for one of the little people of whom all cultures speak. I didn't smell the reputed stink of toe-jam that is supposed to accompany them. I never told the group of what I had seen. There was so much weird stuff happening, that to report another marvel could almost seem like boasting. Only a few days earlier Steve, Marcelle's actor husband, had slept out in the bush and been wakened by an invisible hand touching him in the dark and the sound of Aboriginal voices talking fluently in a Nyoongar language.

My Aboriginal friends think us whitefellas mad to wander the bush at night, yet I am drawn to darkness and mystery. A few years later I picked up an old Aboriginal man and gave him a lift from the east coast of Australia to the west, across the Nullarbor. Out on the plain I camped out while he slept in the car. I discovered that he locked himself in each night. He explained he was scared of kadaitcha man, or Featherfoot. Being on strange country he was unsure if he was welcome, and had no possibility of asking permission. In his reality the spirits will kill or torment a stranger in a strange land. I pointed out that a locked door and glass windscreen was scant protection from kadaitcha. He sheepishly agreed, but kept locking the door.

I slept peacefully outside. I always do. Recently in the Kimberley my companions were tormented by the spirits. Rocks were thrown onto our shade-house roof throughout the night. I heard them, and felt my companions' fear, but knew it had nothing to do with me. I was safe. Most whitefellas are safe. Without belief the magic doesn't penetrate our thick skins.

The Other Side

Soon after I returned from Townsville and my belated grieving for Paul, my friend Polly was rehearsing a play when she suddenly had to bolt from the room and vomit for no apparent reason. She had not been feeling ill or stressed, and then up it came and floored her. It was just after two in the afternoon.

At that moment, on the other side of the city, I was running late for a blood donation and very aware of the time. Because I was lost, I had a good look around the empty street before hurrying down a driveway to ask for directions. That's when things started to get a little weird. It was as if I was running through snow. Of course it was nothing like snow; it was a beautiful warm day. But the space around me had a quality of snowscape, a deadening of sound — a crisp clarity — and a sense of being alive. I was strangely alone in a courtyard, and I turned a number of times, stepping off in several directions without actually going anywhere, before I saw a man through a window. I made my way to him, he gave simple directions, and I walked back out onto the street. No more than a minute or two had elapsed, but where before there had been an empty footpath, now there lay a body, with people around it signalling that life was over.

He lay with his back to me, a large man passed on. Medical officers arrived. I shivered and hurried on.

That evening I heard that Polly had lost her brother. I visited her and discovered that he had collapsed during the afternoon in front of the hospital. I realised at once that it had been her brother John that I had seen. Had I not entered that strange snowy space, I would surely have seen him fall and would have had to deal with his death. It was as if I was spared that anguish and led away. I was able to console Polly a little with confirmation that John had died quickly without suffering. My pinpointing of the time confirmed without doubt that she had vomited at the exact time that her beloved brother departed. It was more proof for me of spiritual connections.

A few weeks later at a large Nyoongar funeral I met a stranger. It had been a long day of dealing with tragic loss for all of us. Theo Kearing was a great Nyoongar, a tireless worker for his people and a mad bastard to boot. He died young and healthy, which is always a crying shame, and left a large, grieving family.

After a long, hot and triumphant memorial march through town, and after the service and burial, a Middar (corroboree) was held in the bush. As well as an activist and organiser, Theo had been a dancer and actor, and his old dance company performed as the sun set through the trees on a favourite piece of his land. His favourite dance was performed by some of the older dancers who had toured with him to Europe and the Americas. It was a comic narrative, and our laughter joined the calling of the magpies. A fitting end to Theo's parting.

Afterwards I walked behind some trees to relieve myself. A stranger joined me. As we pissed he told me that this was the first funeral he had been to in over six months. For an Aboriginal that is a relatively long gap, as large extended families have many members to lose. However, there was a reason for him telling me this and I waited for him to tell me more. I sensed he needed to talk.

'I was sitting at home with the missus,' he explained, 'when suddenly I went cold and shivered so hard I dropped my beer on the floor. I wasn't pissed or nothing, but I went all weird, all of a sudden. And then I knew, something awful had happened to my kids. They were in Adelaide with their mum, and I tried phoning, I was desperate. I just knew. I got woke up the next morning with a phone call. Both of 'em dead.'

His kids' funeral had been the last he had attended. They died cruel deaths, accidentally trapped in a car on a hot day, and he was trying to recover from the shock, loss and anger. He had apparently been in tears most of the day as this funeral kept reminding him of the last one.

'People keep coming up and telling me to pull myself together, that Uncle Theo wouldn't want me to get so upset. But it's not Uncle Theo I'm crying for, it's my babies.' He wanted to know how long the grief would continue, when he would be free of it. I was lost for words at first. Words seem so useless in the face of such calamity, but this stranger seemed to need something from me. I told him I doubted that parents ever fully overcome the tragic loss of children, and that he would always miss his kids and be angry at their untimely death. However, it was likely he would learn how to deal with it and that if he gave it a chance, life would bring new joys.

With a tough smile he stood strong again, as if he had just needed somebody, even a stranger like me, to understand the true depths of his grief. He had no reason to lie to me, no reason to tell me his story at all, except to unburden himself, and I was left with the certainty that he told me the truth. Somehow he had known his kids were dead long before he had received the official message. He had some sort of spiritual connection with his children that transcended the geographical distance between them.

It set me thinking. Most of my defining spiritual moments have been the result of travels to exotic climes and cultures. It is unlikely that many people share such experiences. However, there is one spiritual experience we must all confront. Death.

When I was a kid death disturbed me because my parents tried to protect me by hiding me from funerals and mourning. Grandma West died next door and was spirited away in a big black car in the night. We weren't even supposed to watch it drive away. I was left with a morbid worry. Grandma would either be burnt or eaten by worms. The options terrified me. But I couldn't talk about it. We didn't talk about death.

Lynn and I had often discussed our responsibilities to our children in this area. We had always been open about matters of sex, but were unsure what to do with death. It's not the sort of thing you raise over the dinner table. Walking around the house naked helps to discuss human biology, but you can't invoke the walking dead to educate the kids about their mortality.

When Nyoongar Uncle Eddie Bennell died we had an opportunity. We were invited to view this gentle man at the funeral parlour and decided to take the kids. Eddie was an Aboriginal playwright I had worked with and befriended. Ren and Nina (who were seven and four) knew their Uncle Eddie well and liked him, but his passing was no great trauma for them.

We let the kids know that they could leave at any time, and monitored their reactions carefully. We entered the chill room and walked to the coffin. Eddie was stretched out in a better suit than I'd ever seen him wear. As I looked down my first thought was, 'Eddie never wore that colour lipstick.' He looked liked a waxwork dummy with purple lips. Obviously the undertakers had little experience with black faces. Nina was unsettled and Lynn took her out. Ren looked for a while longer.

'It's not Uncle Eddie,' he finally said, and we left. In the car we discussed where Eddie was now. It was clear to all of us, kids and adults, that the spirit-which-was-Eddie had left. I still have no idea where it went, or what it blended into, but gone it was. The kids had no dark worries of worms or fire. It didn't matter; it was only a wax dummy that was committed to the soil.

I remembered another funeral with kids, lots of kids. Old Mickey Ashton was a star of vaudeville and circus when young, but had ended up as an old drunk on the showground circuit. He was rescued and given a job training young children in acrobatics in the country town of Albury-Wodonga. These last few years were a joy to him, and his little apprentices at the Flying Fruit Fly Circus loved him dearly. When Mickey passed away many of the parents wanted to keep their children away from the funeral but the kids rebelled. When ten children, aged six to sixteen, stood in the church struggling through their tears to deliver a few lines of love to the ancient acrobat, we all balanced on the edge of an emotional volcano.

Most of us got lost on the way to the cemetery. Fifty cars squealing around in circles and asking directions at the butchers shop on the corner. For the old vaudeville star it was the perfect comedy, a Keystone Cops funeral.

At the graveside we participated in an old circus tradition. Instead of soil we dropped sawdust and sparkle into the grave as we said our last farewells. More tears. More anguish.

Back at circus headquarters the adults drank to Mickey's memory, and the kids played on the circus equipment. Within ten minutes all of the circus children were swinging, leaping, bouncing and balancing, laughing and shouting. The sadness had passed; they had grieved deeply, said goodbye and rejoined the circus of life.

In PNG death is treated differently from in the west. There is the same need to grieve and celebrate a life well lived, but also a sense of fittingness which we have lost. It is right to die when one's life has run its course. Old people even decide when they have finished and just pop off. When I first met him Poppa Doiki was dying, but then he discovered more things he had to do and pulled himself together and lived another decade. He was quite clear about what he had done. There is no question in PNG that spirits live on after death; it is taken as a truism. After Launi's bizarre strip the night Poppa died, I had no doubts myself.

It is young death, tragic death, unnecessary death, which they abhor. They believe that if one dies before the time is right, before the spirit has accepted the journey, the spirit can become angry or confused. The sites of car accidents and other untimely deaths are avoided until a shaman can placate the released spirit and send it on.

Every culture, through every period, has developed a belief system about death. Two of the most popular paradigms in my culture are the old-fashioned Heaven and Hell, and the ultra-modern Great Nothingness. Neither of them do much for me but there are so many others to choose from these days. The array of beliefs available on the internet is truly amazing. World religions, cults, traditional concepts and New Age discoveries offer an almost infinite variety of possibilities of afterlife.

There are scientific rationalists I greatly admire who know in their hearts that there is no afterlife. They are rock-solid sure that when they die their light is snuffed. They are reconciled to that and happy, it seems. But I do not have their certainty, and I am glad. I don't want certainty of annihilation. If I am given the opportunity to watch death approach I'd rather it have a taste of adventure, an excitement about what is to occur. If I'm wrong and the scientists are right, and I slam into nothingness, I haven't lost anything.

No one, no religious leader or guru or Nobel Prize winning scientist can be certain of what occurs to us when we shuffle off this mortal coil. To believe you have the only answer is arrogant bullshit. Better, I think, to behave well in case there is a judgement or karmic reward, and keep your options open.

At times, I believe death is the final taboo of the west. The last subject it is forbidden to openly discuss, or lampoon or mention to children. We hide it away in ambulances and funeral parlours, list it in newspapers, pretend it will never happen to us and pray it will never happen to our loved ones.

When confronted with death our wonderful modern views of the world can crumble. Our science is of no use, nor our political beliefs, wealth or social position. We feel suddenly helpless in a chaotic world, insignificant in an uncaring universe. Each death of a loved one we live through, takes us on this journey of the soul, this coming to terms with the vastness of it all and our own feeble flame. Spiritual and religious belief offers meaning in these dire times. It is often hard for cynics and non-believers to shake off a sneaking want-to-believe-in-something-more-majestic when a loved one lies dead before them. Is this really all there is? Gradually we heal again, and shut the door on the awe and re-immerse into the material.

Stone

A completely different ribbon of experience began for me in the isolated wheat belt of South Australia. It was a low point in my life. Lynn and I had remained apart and she wished to move back east. I was determined to remain close to the kids, so until she put down roots I followed at a distance and was homeless. I accepted a job on the Eyre Peninsula of South Australia, developing a vast community arts celebration across thousands of square miles of wheatfields and jagged coastline. I lived in an old cottage in the tiny town of Wudinna, and earned my living a good eighteen hours' drive from my family to the east, or my friends to the west. I was lonely, and not impressed by my own company, but there were benefits to the forced isolation. Time to contemplate my life so far and find a little perspective, to discover my innermost feelings and all those other things that most men find so hard. I find self-improvement as difficult as the next bloke does.

One Sunday, feeling stir crazy, I drove out through the dreary landscape. After millions of years of erosion former mountain ranges have been turned into a dusty plain, which in turn has been flattened by bullock teams and tractors. I was pulled towards the district's most compelling feature, a large granite outcrop reputed to be the second largest granite monolith in the country. It was pretty bloody impressive. I may not be overly sensitive to my own feelings, but I try to be to those of others, and I was pretty certain that this rock would have had spiritual significance to the indigenous people, none of whom now lived in the area. Before venturing onto the weatherworn slopes I introduced myself to the rock, pledged my respect and asked permission to climb. Yes, I spoke to the rock. For me it's the right thing to do.

From the top the farms stretched for miles towards distant blue ranges. The wind, lost and weak in the scrub below, blew strongly in my face and chased away the flies. And the sky was so deep it chased away my blues. A wedge-tailed eagle rode a cross-current, flying seemingly backwards until it pinned me in its shadow. No bullshit, it flew backwards until it shielded me from the sun, and then hovered. I stood in the middle of eagle shadow on the roof of the world.

It was one of those moments when you suddenly become the centre of the universe. When the mechanics of the world stop making logical sense. The eagle hovered. Enraptured, I watched it spiral upwards until it blended into the blue. I lay down in a warm and sheltered rock basin. I breathed.

Slowly in — silence — slowly out — silence — slowly in —

Something seemed to shift. Under my back, in full view of a farmhouse and a picnic ground, the earth seemed to open. The rock didn't tear asunder. I just felt a hole beneath my back and a flow of energy around my body. It came in through a gap in my lower spine, into my kidney fat and then throughout my body. Or so I imagined. I don't know why I imagined kidney fat, I don't even know if there is such a thing. I'd just heard blackfellas talk about it and it seemed to describe the stuff I was feeling.

At first it felt utterly relaxing, and I sank deeper into the rock and began to sense everything around me. But soon there was too much energy coming in. I wondered what I was dabbling with. I started getting hotter whilst the rock stayed cool. I became a little scared, and then more so, and that broke the connection. I stood up and went home, wondering how much I had imagined.

That night I awoke in pain. Knives turned in my back and I threw my body around the house, draped it over furniture and curled it into balls in an effort to stem the agony. It got worse and worse. I tried a hot shower, but the old taps needed a gentle hand and I couldn't get the temperature right, and then took so long climbing out of the bath I was frozen once I was free. I shivered under my doona, thrashing around for comfort, then fell onto the carpet. I had no phone, and no immediate neighbours, and the nearest doctor was an hour away. Somehow I got dressed, but outside the stars started to spin and I dropped to my knees and vomited onto the grass. Now the knives were serrated and blunt, and they were turning circles. My back muscles spasmed, my legs kicked out and I grunted a cry of pain.

Then a pop, then peace.

The stars hung bright and silent. I couldn't believe I was no longer in agony, that relief could be so abrupt. I gulped the night air deeply, and wondered what was wrong with me. I thought about death and how I missed my kids. I had a bloody good cry, then calmed and saw again the stars. And felt the earth turning slowly beneath me.

Gradually a kind of energy flowed again, as it had on

the rock, but this time it was gently warming and it flowed through my back, up my spine, and into my head. I was strangely aware of the ludicrous nature of my position, lying half dressed with a teary face, on the front lawn of a small town cottage, connecting to the underworld. Indeed, it was as if I was connected to some cosmic modem, for into my brain flowed the most extraordinary thoughts and images.

I walked inside and wrote and drew pictures. They describe, in an odd fevered way, an alter-energy cosmology which sort of explains how everything is. That there is not just our reality but others of weird and marvellous possibilities, and all this in a sort of quasi-science involving mass and energy ratios. 'If $E = MC^2$, and the speed of light is a constant, worlds within our world with higher energy will have material beings with less mass.' And other such pearls of weird wisdom. I had thought of none of this before. It poured out of me unbidden and unprompted, and from no source I could fathom. It poured out until I collapsed into sleep … only to wake again in agony.

Again the acrobatics of attempted pain relief until I stumbled outside and endeavoured to drive to the doctor-less hospital on the other side of town. I couldn't get the key in the hole, the stars were dancing chaotically and nausea was rising as the Southern Cross set. The lights of a car meandered down the road and I pulled myself into the beam and desperately flagged it down. An elderly woman peered at me through the pre-dawn gloom and took pity on my pain ravaged face.

The night nurse was full of concern and lay me out on a bed and phoned the distant doctor. He prescribed a painkilling shot and the gentle nurse unlocked a cabinet and prepared a syringe. Left alone for a few minutes, safe in the white womb, I burst into silent tears of relief.

There was a pop, then peace. The pain evaporated as Ms Nightingale approached with her needle. I accepted the jab and slept deeply.

Next morning there was blood in my urine, and by Thursday I was in a bigger town and in the hands of doctors and technicians being injected with dye and bombarded by X-rays and ultrasounds. What did they find? An eight-millimetre stone within my kidney. A decent size, apparently, but it seemed to me a minute thing to have caused so much trouble. I just had a kidney stone. There was nothing to worry about. Apart from the agony returning, but that possibility was sidestepped and best ignored.

Back in my little cottage I stared at the pad of mad scribbles I had written during the long night of agony. A mess of strange drawings and phrases which I half understood. There were patterns and meanings, a glimmer of sense. I consigned it all to pain-induced hallucination and a wild imagination.

While waiting for an appointment with a kidney boffin in Adelaide I got on with my work, which entailed driving hundreds of kilometres of dirt roads. I suffered occasional bouts of pain and nausea, but my biggest physical problem was a pain in the small of my back. It was not a direct result of the stone, but caused more by the worry and stress and inability to get relaxed and fit. The constant driving had my spine locked within muscle spasm and whenever I shifted position it hurt like hell. When I arrived at my destination, I had to crawl out of the driver's seat like an old man and pull myself upright with my arms. I would lean on the roof of the car for a few minutes as I slowly massaged the lower vertebrae and tried to stand. Then I would limp into the meeting and, rather than sit, lean against a wall as I listened and advised.

By the weekend I was a physical mess. I lay on my bed and for hours I stared at my cosmic graffiti. It started to make sense. It seemed to describe alternative energy realities on earth that mingled in certain places. If the vision were true it might explain a red flickering light that soared over a mountain and how Poppa Doiki could spirit fly. I got lost in it all for a night or two. In a strange fever I thought perhaps I had stumbled onto, been given, been shown, the essential truth of existence. Briefly it became crystal clear and I was able to make sense of worldly reality and feel calm at the centre of my being.

Then I became scared of the ramifications. What if it were true? What if I had stumbled onto something rich? Something that would help scientists to unify their theory of everything. Perhaps it would make me famous. Perhaps I would be ridiculed by my friends. Perhaps it's all bullshit. Perhaps.

For a day or two, in that lonely cottage in the wheat belt, I descended into madness. Or came close to enlightenment. The kidney stone brought me back to reality. I had to drive to Adelaide to see a specialist and, once I escaped the house and hit the highway, the world got back to normal.

My country doctor had sent me to a man he had trained with, apparently an excellent surgeon who liked to help rural people. Although I did not have private medical insurance my doc thought it likely his teacher might pull some strings and get me immediately into a public hospital. Having to drive eight hundred kilometres into town had to have its rewards. So I visited the specialist with faith that he was a good man, and that my pain and sickness might soon be over. I walked very slowly into his waiting room, my back ablaze with spasm.

Either my doctor had been a very naive student, or the bastard specialist had changed incredibly. His rooms were jammed solid and he dispensed very quick consultations. I disliked his smarmy ways as soon as I saw him, but hid my feelings so as to try to sweet-talk him into a hospital bed. We chatted amiably for a few minutes and he showed me his collection of monstrous kidney stones. Then he led me into the examination room and became suddenly coy as he asked me to lower my undies. He felt my testicles with a revolting revulsion.

I have no problem with nudity or my body, and certainly no problem with a doctor examining my privates. I just expect them to explain what they are doing and then to do it professionally and with care. This bastard said nothing and then pounced as if he were doing something immoral. I felt invaded.

When I said I was a public patient he immediately lost interest in me. Told me I would be placed on the list, and would have to wait a few months.

'What do I do about the pain?'

'Take some painkillers. I find a good bottle of red helps immensely,' he offered as he showed me the door.

I was furious and in pain. I went to the beach and walked out a long pier in the rain. I seethed. I felt impotent and lonely, and a million miles from my family. Friends in Adelaide suggested an acupuncturist and a Chinese herbalist. I rang the acupuncturist. He was unsure if he could help with the stone, but thought he could fix my back pain. I'd had acupuncture a couple of times and found it relaxing and helpful, but I wasn't prepared for the miracle.

Into my back he placed slender needles of the newest steel, and *onto* my back he stuck smoking flasks of vacuum which sucked my flesh into themselves and heated me up. The needles started to quiver, almost hum, as I lay in the darkened room alone. The sickness and the fear of sickness and the work and the endless driving screamed out their cacophony as I lay there. But the cups kept heating things up, and the vileness of the last few weeks and the loneliness and the I-want-my-kids-to-hug sadness all suddenly gave up in a big, warm sigh of I-don't-care. Fuck it all. Let it go. Something weird is happening in my back, but it's not unpleasant and I'm melting across the table. A stranger is looking after me and I feel safe. Something's working so let it go, let it work, drift away.

I sagged and floated in the dark as the cups and needles performed their magic.

The healer returned and slid the needles silently from my flesh. The cups came off with loud pops of expanding skin. He told me to climb off the massage table. It had been so painful getting up onto it that I was very tentative. I negotiated the move very slowly, lowering my legs carefully. I kept expecting a shot of agony but by the time I had my feet on the floor I still felt nothing. Now came the big test — standing erect. It's apparently what differentiates us from the apes. I straightened my spine disc by disc, at every moment expecting a twinge, a stab, a burn. Nothing. I took a few steps around the room.

'You've cured me,' I cried. He demurred, and made another appointment to talk about the stone. I walked out of his house tall and pain free, and stayed that way. The next morning my back felt fine and I had a little jog along the beach. The pain was gone. Well, the immediate, always-there-when-you-moved, really annoying pain was gone.

The kidney stone still lived however, building up its

razor sharp piss-crystals and occasionally trying to make a dash to the bladder. In the centre of Adelaide, on my way to a meeting, I collapsed outside a beautiful museum building. I just had to lie down amid the bustling crowds. I must have seemed like an alcoholic or an addict, judging from the looks the clean burghers of Adelaide gave me as they stepped around my twisting body. I went to find the Chinese herbalist.

Doctor Li was delightful and fun in a brittle Chinese sort of way. She spoke little English, and her helper translated when necessary, but mainly she just felt my pulses, looked into my eyes and recoiled from my tongue. She prescribed an elaborate concoction of herbs and minerals, strange twigs and roots and mushrooms. Her assistant pulled handfuls of the ingredients out of the wooden boxes that lined the walls. He made up six equal piles of what began to look like miniature mountains — with trees and giant mushrooms and fern gardens — bundled them into brown papers and handed them to me.

I had to boil up those magical witch's concoctions in a ceramic kettle and drink the evil looking brew. It was near black and gave off curls of white smoke and stank to high heavens, but strangely I took to its weird taste. I knew it was doing me good, and I spent many hours brewing and drinking the awful muck. My friend nursed me and when I returned to the wheat belt everyone was astounded by my health.

They all said I looked well. I felt well. I could use my tongue again in polite company; it was clean of the yellow scud. I woke up feeling refreshed and looking forward to the day. My energy returned and I thought I had licked the bastard ball of calcium. I got back to work. I searched the Internet for kidney stone information. I discovered the Chinese equate kidney troubles with fear, and that western medicine has mixed ideas about what causes the stones. Stress, inadequate water consumption and bad diet seem likely contributors.

I began to build a history of the stone in my head. I assigned its birth to PNG, to the time when I often lacked plentiful, pure fresh water, laboured under great expectations and stress, and suppressed a great deal of fear. Fear of my kids' constant sicknesses, of mud slides and car accidents and weekly earth tremors. I even believed I pinpointed the very weeks when the pebble began its growth: the night of the blood-piss followed by the *'don't show fear'* hour with the new administrator. I began to believe that the core of my stone was pure PNG.

I finally had the courage to look again at my mad revelations. They set me thinking. The multiverse they described, if true, could explain the sorcery in Oropot, Poppa's ability to astral travel, and a flying fox spirit in the clouds. I didn't allow myself to take the scribbles seriously, but it was from this point that I began to recollect the moments of the weird and wonderful in my life. As I continued to travel the Eyre Peninsula I sat in motel rooms and wrote of Papua New Guinea and Popeye PK. Out of the pain and isolation this book began to grow.

The first phase of the Eyre Peninsula job came to an end. I lived with the kids in Canberra, while Lynn roamed the east coast searching for a new home. Eventually Ren and Nina's nostalgia for friends in Fremantle convinced Lynn to give the West another chance. We all drove back across the Nullarbor and I found work with a puppet company, and then won a major fellowship which gave me funds to research, write and direct a number of plays. My knees actually buckled when I heard the news — two years without financial worry, confirmation of the quality of my work and a chance to hone my craft. Life seemed to be getting back on track.

But deep inside the piss-crystals kept growing and sharpening their blades around the surface of my kidney stone. The stone bided its time and lurked, turning occasionally to remind me of its presence. Finally the call from Royal Perth Hospital came and new X-rays showed the same little white ball of obstructiveness still lurking. I agreed to undergo ultrasound therapy. Modern technology had a second chance.

As they lay me down in a warm bath of water and positioned electrodes near my nipples, it seemed as if my own personal journey from scientist to believer in 'the other' was being played out in my own body. Would strange roots and leaves and needles from China prove more effective than million dollar whizzbang machines? Was a mixture of the two the best therapy? Did I need faith in order for the technology to work? How could I empirically test these questions?

Slightly fuzzy from whatever drug the anaesthetist was pumping into my blood I watched in awe as they slid me above a sci-fi ray gun thingy that was meant to smash my stone to smithereens. I was warned that I had to lie completely still, and that some people found the procedure so unpleasant that they had to be knocked out completely. This added an interesting frisson to the experience — would I be strong enough to cope?

It was all very strange. The beeps and whirls of monitors, the underwater sounds of the oxygen mask, the dull hulk of the surrounding machines, the oozy warm unreality of the drugs. A regular flick/click began inside me. Every second or so I heard and felt flick/click, over and over for ten minutes at a time. It felt, and sounded, like someone flicking their finger into my flesh. Flesh deep within my skin. The intensity of the flick/click increased until it became quite painful. I controlled the pain by breathing into it, by examining it in detail. I lay absolutely still and stayed calm.

Every so often they pulled me out, repositioned the sights of the ray gun and began it all again. Flick/click — flick/click — flick/click — flick/click —

After it was over the anaesthetist asked if I had been meditating. I admitted that I had been, sort of, that I had used a breathing exercise to keep calm and in control.

'There was obviously something happening right,' he said. 'Most people's pulse goes up in line with the increased intensity of the energy we fire at you. Your heartbeat remained even throughout.'

This pleased me immensely. There had been a melding of the modern and the ancient, and I felt well and empowered. I pissed a little blood and was allowed home. The next day I felt so well that I went running and swimming. I had been expecting some pain, or at least discomfort, as the pulverised pieces swam down into my bladder and out to pee. I felt nothing. Two weeks later another X-ray showed that the combination of therapies had not cured my malaise. The bastard was still there, strong as ever, grinning at me from the film sheet. 'You don't get rid of me that easily,' it snarled, and I lapsed into despair.

I had to return to the Eyre Peninsula for the second phase of the consultancy. The project was in disarray. Nothing had happened since I had left five months before. I had falsely assumed that in my absence the organising committee and community groups would have debated my recommendations, but there had been no development. The woman who had instigated the project and promised me all sorts of help had left. Both organisations that had set up the project wanted the other to own it. Everything seemed to have been left for me to fix on return. It was my fault as much as anyone's as I had obviously failed to share the responsibility as much as I'd imagined.

Despite the problems there were hundreds of enthusiastic people excited about my return. They were ready to start singing and writing and dancing. I plunged into the work. The stress was back on, and the bastard kidney rumbled. I hadn't had any stone trouble for a couple of months, but back in Wudinna I was aware of it again.

I went back out to the rock, that huge granite outcrop that set off my kidney stone like some cosmic alarm clock nine months before. I hadn't been back since then. I'd kidded myself that I just hadn't got around to revisiting, but it was really a deep fear that had kept me away. Fear of getting into something dangerous which threatened my health.

I was challenged by a book I was reading to 'fear not,' and, as the afternoon was a blissful blue, I drove out through the wheat fields and wandered across the pink rock. I felt trepidation, but everything was peaceful. No eagle this time, just a simple hello and a silent walk.

I roamed the lower rugged ridges, and discovered twisted rocks of beauty, indolent lizards and hidden watercourses. Several families clamoured and clambered across the granite slopes, racing each other to the top. I became philosophical, meditating on the west's cultural imperative to get to the top as quickly as possible. This has been a great strength in terms of domination and wealth, but has brought us in danger of missing the meaning of our being here. Mounting the peak should crown the journey, not reduce the exploration that can be enjoyed upon the way. If you are racing to the top it might be wise to stop and turn around occasionally, to take in the view and give yourself time to catch up.

I sat cross-legged high above the plain, staring out across the scrub to the ranges beyond. The sun warmed the rocks and my face, and I was washed by a gentle breeze. I chose to meditate, to breathe deeply and gently drift. Flies buzzed about, landed in my hair and crawled across my skin. At first I brushed them away, every flick destroying my tranquillity. Then I found the fly meditation. Instead of allowing them to upset me I focused on the sensation of their walking on my flesh. At worst they merely tickled and allowing them to sit seemed to still them. Soon I was at peace.

The sun warmed my face as I looked far across the plain to the Gawler Ranges; a jagged purple scar of raised welts on the ancient skin of Australia.

White streaks of clouds slice the sky,
and cut up the wheatfields with their shadows.
The bees hum, wind hums,
Rock hums deep ...

Sitting in awe of a landscape must be one of the most common of all 'spiritual experiences'. Like vivid starry nights, great vistas shrink most human beings to insignificance and force us to glory in a life so beautiful.

We all need the occasional dose of Paradise.

A few months later, back in Perth, I went in for another shot at stone smashing. Flick/click — flick/click — flick/click — flick/click ...

The next day I felt so well that I was jumping out of my

skin. Bugger! I wanted pain and blood to prove the powdering of my tormentor, but there was nothing.

'Its smaller!' declared the doctor. 'Down to half its size. With any luck one more blast will finish it.'

One more blast took months to organise. Flick/click — flick/click — flick/click — flick/click ... This third session was far more unpleasant than the first two. The anaesthetist must have upped the drugs, because I was less able to control things with my breathing and afterwards I lay for hours in a disorientating fug. I felt crook, so in the crazy reality of kidney stone therapy I assumed that things had gone well.

No such luck. The little white marble still smiled from the X-ray sheet. 'I'm still here!'

The doctors now declared my stone to be a strong little bastard that was not responding to ultrasound. They wanted to go in and fetch it out. Keyhole surgery. Little tubular surgery. Easy-peasy.

Aaaaah. Now I was scared. The only other time I have gone under the scalpel was for the foot tendons I cut in North Queensland. I conned my way into the care of one of Melbourne's best orthopaedic surgeons ('Ortho to the Australian Ballet'), and still picked up a post-op infection. The three tendons he reconnected have performed admirably, but the sickening, putrid foot flesh that fired red train-track lines up my leg into my groin has carved a nasty memory. With love and care it all cleaned up, but I hated to think what a similar mischance would do to my kidney.

It was not that I didn't trust the surgeon to cut and plunge his or her way into my kidney and crush and extract my stone with great aplomb. Nor did I fear that the anaesthetist would let me wake during the op. It was the fear of microbes and mutant germs polluting my interior that kept me awake at night.

I became fit. Acting in a very energetic production helped no end: running around like an idiot twice a day for the pleasure of an audience tends to strip the lazy fat away. I also drank another fetid Chinese witch's brew along with gallons of water.

The night before the operation I played a basketball semi-final. At the post-game barbecue I asked a fellow guard in the team, a student nurse, for advice about being operated on in the morning. At first Aron refused to be drawn into a role of expert. He did, however, have a huge interest in hospital healing arts, having had his arm saved after a massive skateboard injury, and had written a term paper on how patients best heal. He'd found experimental support for the following healing principals:

> Patients who believe that the operation will be successful heal much better than those who doubt the process.
>
> Patients who understand what is happening heal better.
>
> Patients who state their fears heal more quickly than do those who hide them and pretend to be brave.

'So don't be a martyr,' Aron warned. 'The only way the medical staff can help you is if they know what's going on. With internal stuff you're the only one who can inform them. If it hurts tell them.'

I asked him who I should talk to about the procedure.

'You'll probably only get to see the anaesthetist.'

'Not the surgeon?'

'Unlikely. But the anaesthetist is the main man. The surgeon is just doing a very simple procedure and he's just focusing on a few centimetres deep inside your body.

The anaesthetist has the whole picture. He's in control of your life, in waking you and checking bodily signs. Ask anything or tell anything to him. But do it before he sticks the drug in. There's no time after that. They still do the old clichéd 'count back from ten' routine, and nobody gets below five.'

I arrived early at the hospital. In my fetching gown of hospital green I was wheeled into a near empty ward with picture windows overlooking the city.

Then this tall, vivacious, gorgeous woman came and stood by my trolley bed.

'I am your anaesthetist.'

We had a relatively lengthy chat about my concerns and she put me at ease. When I was wheeled into the operating theatre antechamber she opened the door to the inner sanctum and spoke loudly enough for me to hear.

'Our next patient, Phil, was once one of us, a medical student, so let's look after him. He trusts our skills, but he's a bit afraid of post-op infection, so make this one really clean!'

She turned and gave me the thumbs up, and a smile. It made me really happy to know I was being looked after, that my needs were being listened to. It was actually quite odd to feel happy only moments before some stranger would plunge a scalpel into my flesh and then rummage around with a pair of mini-pliers. Yet happy I was.

I was wheeled into the theatre and nodded at the few pairs of eyes that looked down at me from above their masks. Masks and lights, a cast of white-gowned players, it was theatre indeed. I was moved onto the central platform and everyone moved closer. My anaesthetist nodded for a tube to be attached to the back of my hand, and then she turned and faced me. She moved in close.

'We're going to start now Phil,' she smiled. I waited for the count-from-ten routine, but instead she just leaned closer, a beautiful, haloed vision. 'Some people would pay a lot of money for this drug,' she purred, and then split into two. She half grinned as she suddenly fractured into a hundred kaleidoscopic reproductions which in turn exploded like silver fireworks and vanished into velvet blackness.

I awoke in a ward and gradually came to terms with the pain of passing blood clots (oh that sweet morphine) and tubes sticking out of my back and the end of my dick. I was in for a couple of days, not a horrible experience by any means. It was lovely to be nursed and I was happy just to rest. With the stone captured in a phial beside my bed I assumed this story was over.

A few days later I awoke at home in the middle of a mighty electrical storm. My kidney hurt. I tossed and turned for hours as the storm dissipated into dawn and the day heated up into a stinker. The pain continued to get worse, gradually becoming agonising. I assumed it was another blood clot trying to move, but when I realised I had stopped pissing, despite drinking gallons of water, I began to get fearful. I vomited up my painkillers around noon, and my doctor sent me back into hospital.

My father drove me into town, with my mother and daughter as passengers. Every bump or application of brakes along the way sent spasms of pain tracking across my body. I staggered into Emergency like an old man. Within a minute I was being led through the doors. There was time to give Nina one last careful hug. She was being brave and strong, but was obviously dreadfully worried about her agonised dad.

For a few moments I was left in a corridor, but soon I was wheeled into my own cubicle. I lay tight and unmoving, breathing in shallow little gasps. My worries of a post-op complication seemed to be coming true. I felt awful and, when I remembered Nina's anxiety in the corridor, I burst into tears. My body heaved as great sobs and gulps exploded from my chest. In silence (amazing how our conditioning still controls us in moments of major stress) I physically gave up fully to the heaving cry.

Suddenly, there was a strange fizzing sensation at the end of my dick and then a silent pop deep inside me. All pain vanished. I pissed blood and clots for half an hour and then it was all over. I was cured. I went home a couple of hours later and have not had even an echo of pain since.

Having set up my kidney stone saga as somehow symbolic of my understanding of existence and the science/spirituality debate, the final results are kind of interesting. The alternative therapies had eased the symptoms, while ultrasound ray guns had failed. However, it took the technology of microsurgery and anaesthetics to eliminate the rogue rock once and for all, and the final cleansing of the blocks and cure of the pain had come through emotional release. Both science and spirit had healed me. I allowed both to work. I allowed a partnership of the alternatives, of the natural enemies, and I was cured. Victory over my stone seemed to suggest that multiple beliefs and techniques were healthy.

All I had left to remind me of the months of pain and worry was a small scar in my side — and a few pages of mad scribblings. During the unfolding of the saga of the kidney stone I had kept writing stories. Memories of the breathing cave, sacred sites, talk of a gateway in Massi village were fresh in my mind again. I began to write a book, and then my work took me to other places where magic was still free upon the earth.

Thongs and Eagles

In Darwin a new gateway was built. In 1998, four hundred teenagers from around Australia came to investigate the different experiences of white and black and decide what they, our youth, wanted to do for reconciliation. Whilst the majority were non-Aboriginal there were representatives of Aboriginal youth from around Australia, and the blackfellas had a large say in the organising.

I was a guest at this first national youth reconciliation convention; along with three colleagues from Western Australia we were invited to present our production *Bidenjarreb Pinjarra*. This highly successful play is an improvised comedy about the first massacre of Aboriginal people in Western Australia. In 1834 Governor Sir James Stirling led an armed expedition into the territory of the Bidenjarreb Nyoongars on the banks of the Murray River. What was enshrined in history as the Battle of Pinjarra, was in reality a premeditated surprise attack on predominantly women, children and elders by specially trained police and soldiers armed with the latest weaponry. Two Nyoongar and two whitefella actors created the work through improvisation, in an attempt to recreate traditional playmaking techniques. The result has been one of the funniest political works created in Australia. Satire, mime, improvised comedy, dramatic conflict and tough physical theatre, switch the audience between 1834 and the present. The play disarms audiences with its playful improvisation before exploding the battle myths with the full horror of the massacre. A post-show discussion provides time for communal reflection on past tragedies and cultural loss, uniting the audience in a dignified memorial to the fallen. It was a fitting show for the gathering.

The elders of Yirrkala, north-east Arnhem Land, thought the youth convention so significant they decided to create a new ceremony to take to Darwin. A ceremony using ancient rites of food sharing and respect, dance and didge, smoke and chanting. It was the first time these rituals had been performed away from Yirrkala sacred lands. In strange territory, on the lawns of a Catholic college, new land was consecrated. A new gateway was opened.

For two days and nights the ceremonial ground was prepared and sung over. During the day, as I went about my business, they went about theirs. Old men sitting talking low, women walking up and down in lines of swishing arms, sudden flurries of clapstick and boomerang slap, songs snaking through the heavy air. At night I stayed away for the word had been passed around that kadaitcha man might be walking the land. This was communicated through nods and secret smiles and quiet bursts of words: 'Kadaitcha man — he's here — stay clear.' I slept outside, but a good distance from the rituals, and fell in and out of sleep, as bursts of chanting and clapstick floated through the trees. I felt totally secure, but sensed the prowling walk of something powerful guarding the now sacred ground.

On the third night the delegates gathered on the site for rituals of food and fire, chanting and didgeridoo and exhortations to love the land and its people. We sat in long lines facing each other; black facing white, as elders clapping boomerangs paced the perimeter. Didgeridoo spirits sang their ancient drones. Flames lit up long beards and painted chests. Women bit the night with high sharp wails.

Suddenly a mobile phone went off. All four hundred guests, black and white, cringed with shame at what we assumed was sacrilege, and quietly cursed whichever one of us had brought a phone along. Then we laughed with relief on discovering the mobile belonged to one of the dancing elders. He nonchalantly pulled the phone from his traditional clothing and answered his call. I discovered later that the call was from an important elder far away who, unable to attend through sickness, was checking that his part of the ceremony was being properly performed. Thus the ancient rites were sustained via modern technology.

We shared food, listened and watched in silence. A wonderful didgeridoo player, a young man, but a powerful presence all night, talked in poetic English about the land. Bursts of passionate speech in the rhythm of song. Then an elder spoke in his language. His poetry swirled and soared. We understood not one word, but everything he said. We were welcome, we had responsibility, we must respect, we must learn to live side by side. We were all humbled. The spirits were abroad and four hundred young people were in awe. Most had never guessed at such power and beauty, never understood how precious were the old ways, never felt such love for their country before. They were ready to reconcile.

On the final night of the convention the delegates were

to present their plan for the nation, and we were to perform our comic take on the nation's tragic past. Also on the bill were the Yirrkala dancers from the ceremony. They came backstage already dressed and painted so were not allocated a dressing room. I noticed an old woman beginning to jiggle and suggested to my fellow performers that we move into one dressing room and give the other, with its toilet, to the women. They dived into the dunny with great enthusiasm. The male dancers used our facilities. We began talking and a young dancer quietly told us that at least one of the senior dancers was kadaitcha, a spirit man.

After their performance the Yirrkala mob left the theatre, and when I returned to my dressing room after our performance I found a pair of blue rubber thongs left on my clothes in my corner. I didn't know if the shoes had any significance to whoever left them. It probably wasn't the kadaitcha, I told myself, but they did have lightning bolts printed on them.

I thought we might meet up with the dancers later that night so took the thongs back to our camp. I was mistaken; they had already gone bush. Nobody in Darwin wanted the thongs. Most thought them worthless and inconsequential (despite their perfect condition). Some blackfellas felt them dangerous and suggested I leave them in the bin. I tried them on. Beautiful fit. The colour matched my eyes. I brought them home.

I had what might be the thongs of the kadaitcha man, and didn't know if I should wear them. Despite seemingly being left where I could find them, and fitting like Cinderella's slippers, I only dared put them on for seconds at a time. I was drawn to their potency but held myself back from dancing in them.

Before I found the nerve, or stupidity, I was back in South Australia for one last attempt to direct the Eyre Peninsula project. I took an afternoon off and found an isolated beach. As I ran through the sand I disturbed a pair of sea eagles who took to the wing with long, sliding glides. After a swim and a search through rock pools at the far end of the bay I jogged back towards my car. Once again the eagles soared up from the sand. One headed out across the waves but the other slowly cruised the shore in front of me. I was thrilled to share the beach with this magnificent bird, and held my arms out to mimic its wings and flapped in unison with it. A silly thing to do, perhaps, but nobody was watching and I felt like flying.

The bird dipped a wing and slowly turned. I did the same. It flew back towards me as I jogged back the way I'd come. I dipped my wing and turned back, to find the bird had mimicked me. I spun a figure of eight; it followed, drawing ever closer. For several marvellous minutes we danced together, the bird flying only feet in front of my right shoulder. At times it led the pas de deux, at times it followed me. A graceful, swooping dance that left me swooning breathlessly when finally the magnificent bird flew off to join its mate.

Back in Fremantle, I sat one afternoon trying to write but it was stinking hot and my mind was wandering. Some impulse took me outside, where above the garden a sea eagle hovered for quite some minutes. I had never known sea eagles out the back of Fremantle. I've hardly ever seen the beasts anywhere before, except for that afternoon near Streaky Bay. But here it was, looking for its dance partner. Well, it wasn't of course. Streaky Bay was some two thousand kilometres to the east, and I hadn't left my address. But it looked like the same bird and I indulged my fantasy and danced for it across the lawn.

That afternoon a friend phoned, inviting me to join her at her parent's holiday home in Lancelin for the weekend. 'You'll love it,' Christine enthused, 'the bird life is extraordinary.'

'Any sea eagles?'

'I don't think so. I don't think I've ever seen sea eagles here. Why?'

'There'll be some there when I arrive!'

The audacity of my prediction puzzled me but I felt strangely confident. I felt that there might well be a sea eagle awaiting me.

And there was. Two of them. A couple which took to the wing from the town beach as we ran towards them. All the next day they wheeled past our beach house as if they were looking in the window, looking for me. I struggled to find some meaning to the raptor occurrences.

Near Streaky Bay, I had danced with the eagle because I allowed myself. I allowed myself to follow a strange impulse to spread my arms and fly with the bird. Allowed myself to be foolish and mad, and gained a joyful experience. And when I met another eagle over my back yard I allowed the possibility that it was not just a weird coincidence and had taken it to suggest we would meet again. I allowed the possibility of future contact to occur, and even predicted it. I allowed the possibility that the birds would be in Lancelin and they were.

I went to the window and spoke to them. I whispered, 'I allowed your possibility and now you are,' as they passed the window once more. Contented they dipped their wings, spun on the tips and tacked against the breeze as they headed out to sea. I swear it seemed as if they'd heard me and, satisfied I'd got the message, they headed off for home.

I didn't see a sea eagle again for quite a while. But I

developed a new philosophy. *That which is allowed can come to pass. That which is denied has no bloody hope.*

It's obvious, really. If you don't buy a lottery ticket you cannot possibly win; if you buy one you have a chance. The missionary wraps his spirit behind biblical armour and cannot be harmed by sorcery, while a young village girl succumbs to powdered bone being blown upon her. It all depends on what you will allow. If you allow magic, it can be used. If you allow love it can be shared. If you allow UFOs they can be seen. If you allow adventure it can be had.

Perhaps this explains why cynics and scientists can never find proof of the supernatural. Since they don't believe, they cannot see; what they can't allow can never happen. Their experiments will always draw a blank. Magic cannot occur under the cold disbelieving gaze of the unbeliever.

I was never attracted to organised religion partly because my contemporary sensibilities could not cope with the concept of faith. I remember as a young man laughing at the concept that you needed faith to see Jesus. To see Him you first needed to believe, but my scientific orthodoxy demanded I see something before I could believe in it. My science disallowed the circular arguments of faith, but now I was beginning to argue those very same circularities. My experiences suggest that whether it is Jesus, Mohammed, Krishna or a garden god, fairies, angels, astral travellers or UFOs, if you allow the possibility, they may exist. If you close your mind, they have no chance.

I fear that the rational certainty of the techno-west will simply not allow the magnificent possibilities of human spiritual endeavour to flourish. Without proof, science consigns so many possibilities to the rubbish bin. You could call it the Tinkerbell Principle: every time someone says, 'I don't believe,' a fairy dies. I fear for what we are losing.

These thoughts tumbled as I drove back to Fremantle. When I walked into my bedroom the thongs were waiting for me, or that's how it seemed to me. They grabbed my attention and I sat with them on my lap, wondering if my new philosophy of allowance could be put to the test. I had allowed a string of snake's vertebrae to wield a strange power and my Poppa allowed his spirit to roam the world without passport or airline ticket. I had discovered for myself that ancient cultures were able to imbue everyday objects with magic, and that the power is bloodcurdlingly real. The question was — dare I allow a pair of second-hand thongs to let me fly?

The problem with universal allowing is that it can lead you into scary territory. I started to worry. If I allow that UFOs can exist, might I be plucked from my bed by aliens and have horrid probes poked up my nose? If I allow a spirit world, will I start being bothered by poltergeists? Once the lid is opened dangerous possibilities abound.

It is so much safer to cling to the familiar. Most Australians are either benign Christians or materialists who don't believe in any of this bullshit. Most Aussies enjoy a simple, safe and prosperous life and have no need to unveil frightening possibilities. There is no need to open Pandora's Box when you have faith in your future and food in your belly. Ignorance is bliss.

I almost put the thongs away, but the adventurer within me outvoted the pragmatic coward. I decided to dance in the thongs of the kadaitcha, and see if I could fly like an eagle. I went outside. I sat in the park opposite my house and meditated on the shoes in my hands, allowing them power. For a microsecond I swear I lifted, the grass tilted and a vista lay below me. I saw the dark park and street lighting dropping away. But I panicked and fell to earth. Not with a jolt, but it took my breath away just the same. I ran indoors. I turned on lights and the television and tried to act normal. I had allowed the thongs a power that fascinated and attracted me, but when I turned it on I was filled with fear.

The next night they moved of their own volition. While I was out of the room for a few moments they moved from the floor to the table. I did not move them and nobody else was at home. I never put shoes on the table. Over the course of several tours, Aboriginal actor Shorty Parfitt had drummed into me that to do so was very bad luck. I had stopped doing it. The thongs seemed to have jumped up by themselves.

Either I was going mad or I was dabbling with dangerous things. I remembered Launi telling me that I had nothing to fear from the spirit world as long as I didn't dabble with it. Playing with the thongs felt like dabbling. Having almost flown once I was beginning to believe that if I danced in them I might enter the world of the supernatural. But if I did that, I would lose the ignorance which protected me. I wanted to stop dabbling but I was hooked. I was scared of getting lost in the labyrinths of possibility, but I kept daring myself to dance again. Phil Thomson — Thong Test Pilot. Did I have the right stuff?

I remembered the gateway Launi had worried about. Perhaps it was the way into the village for me if I got my thongs to fly. These gateways may be the stations on the astral network through which adepts can enter and exit our concrete reality. I wondered where the nearest gateway was to suburban Fremantle. The idea of flying through space was deeply attractive, though I feared what beasties from other realms I might encounter should I find a way to open a door.

Despite the fear I decided to dance. I went far away from the suburbs out into the bush. I chose a full moon, and took with me an array of magic objects — the thongs, a large Ramu River men's carving, a lump of balga gum, my Wudinna scribblings and my kundu drum.

I found a level circular space beside a creek and blessed it with smoking gum, asking for support and forgiveness for what I was trying to do. I sat up all night thinking, singing, dancing and reading. I grappled to find awe in the firmament. The stars were vivid, but failed that night to move my soul. I shuffled around in a circle and tried a few chants. It felt horribly American New Age Warrior and I almost went home in embarrassment. But I settled down and sat and meditated. I breathed deeply and slowly, and gradually duplicated the rhythms of the cave.

Slowly in — silence — slowly out — silence — slowly in —

I should have just left it at that, a nice peaceful time filling me with calm strength. But I had to keep pushing ahead. I had to see the dare through. So I placed the thongs upon my feet and started to dance. I shudder still to see the image of me turning slow circles and stamping my feet into the earth desperate to make a connection. Poor misguided fool!

It got worse. With no response from the thongs or heavens I put the 'magic' shoes upon my hands and ran around like Superman. Arms outstretched, willing myself up into the air. Oh dear.

And when the dawn came riding through the trees I knew at last that whatever magic I had tasted in my life was not at my beck and call. I do not have the power to make magic in the night at will, nor to choose a destination and simply take flight. No matter how much I allow the mysterious to be, it will not manifest on my demand. I am of this world and lack the knowledge and training to enter into another.

I returned home tired. The fever was spent. I no longer wanted to fly. The idea of me evoking suburban magic seemed funny, and I fell asleep laughing at myself. I tossed the thongs into the cupboard with other ordinary shoes.

I thought I had finished with all the foolishness.

India

It is perhaps a little strange that I had never visited India. Living on the shores of the Indian Ocean one is very aware of the mysterious subcontinent lying to our north. All my adult life I have been aware of people flying to India to find the mystical answers to life's conundrums. At first it was the Beatles, growing flowing beards and sitting with gurus, who attracted my attention to the land of the Hindu. Then friends started leaving the safety of home to adventure through the east. They came back thin and full of tales of teeming millions and wandering cattle. Then I became aware of a new wave of spiritual seekers,visiting Poona and the Himalayas in search of ancient wisdom and fulfilled lives.

I remember arguing with friends in the eighties that they should stay at home and discover the spiritual in the red earth of their own country. My cynicism saw through the poppycock of priests and I didn't feel comfortable with the concept of the guru. I had been encouraged by the media to equate eastern mysticism with fat millionaires and hated to see my friends seduced by such nonsense. When acquaintances returned smiling and calm I feared the influence of cults, although I am not sure why I was so worried by my friends being happy. Later I realised that many intelligent people had benefited deeply by their exposure to India and its culture. I stopped being afraid, but still wasn't drawn personally.

Last year I had the opportunity to visit. Daksha Sheth, an Indian dancer and choreographer, and David Pye, an Australian composer, had set up a collaboration to develop a work based on the ancient Gilgamesh epic, and I was invited to participate as a writer. I was offered a free trip and the chance to work with a dance company on the shore of a lake in southern India. I would have the opportunity to study Indian comic storytelling and witness traditional temple performance. Not surprisingly I said yes.

This was not to be the hard Indian experience of many travellers. We were looked after from the moment we landed, given clean quarters and a superb local cook to feed us. Working with a company of dancers ensured an easy entry into the culture. New friends showed us around and answered our questions.

Whilst not on the search for personal enlightenment I was intrigued by the spiritual and religious beliefs of this country I was visiting. I wondered what evidence I might garner for my new theories on allowance and whether I might witness oriental magic.

I could not avoid contact with manifestations of Hindu culture. Despite Kerala being a democratically elected communist state, the old religions are still pumping strong. I stayed next door to the temple of a female deity. Before supplicants can present their gifts and pray for blessing and relief from their particular earthly woes, they must first ensure she is wide-awake and attentive. With so many people on this crowded continent needing godly help it is imperative to grab her attention from the outset. The answer is to make lots of noise. There is drumming and the clang of gongs, and the ricochet pings of cymbals and bells. To bolster the bedlam acolytes chant and banks of high-tech speakers blast Hindi movie music. Bursts of firecrackers split the noise in half and try to wake the dead. Four times a day, from early morning to late evening.

One day I sit with a Hindu dancer and her one-legged Moslem husband. They are intelligent and modern in outlook and grimace at the sounds of the temple. I ask them about their religious beliefs and the difficulties of their mixed marriage. They tell me their marriage has not attracted persecution. With the sabre waving and nuclear brinkmanship between India and Pakistan, I am glad that, at least in the more relaxed Kerala, people can fall in love across religious barriers. I see hope in that.

Because India is famous for its spiritual knowledge I begin to quiz Mochitha and Reji. They profess to be intrigued by such questions from westerners. They don't think much about such things. It's not important to their living. However, they both have a basic belief in the recycling of the spirit. Neither the mild Moslem nor moderate Hindu have any doubt that spirit continues after death, that this existence is just part of a great cycle. It is a given in their lives. Spiritual questions are thus of no great concern to them as all the answers will come in the fullness of time.

Believing in an afterlife, paradise or in a cycle of lives seems pretty wacky to many of us in the west, yet in India it is almost universal. Over my stay I became convinced that it is the underlying strength of basic spiritual belief that allows this powerful nation to thrive. The millions of squatter dwellers in the cardboard and packing-case shanties that crowd Mumbai, do not exhibit the despair one tends to associate with such terrible poverty. Neither is there much obvious conflict, despite the huge disparities between rich and poor. At least that was my observation. I guess that anger at one's lowly station in life may be dissipated by the knowledge that this is just one existence out of many.

The poorest of Australian suburbs are rich in comparison with the vast majority of Indian communities, yet I am much more aware of explosive anger and personal frustration in my home country. Graffiti stains our walls; drugs and alcohol destroy our lives. When you only believe in one life on this planet it is one hell of a bitch if you find yourself poor and without prospects.

The concept of religion as the opiate of the masses was one I understood well as a young man. It fired up my youthful political fervour and confirmed in my mind that science promised a more equal world than we had under the yoke of powerful religions. The lives of millions of poor had been made bearable by priests' promises of eternal life, but this also discouraged them from overthrowing the rich few who exploited their work. Religion propped up dictators and held the masses in check. The rationalist, humane world of the future, which replaced primitive nonsense with scientific certainty, would become a celebration of human equality. Such were my youthful beliefs.

Of course I had not predicted the ravages of economic rationalism or recognised the power of greed. Relaxing religious morality and the fear of a final reckoning has allowed more individuals to sidestep communal responsibility and focus on developing personal wealth. Greed is celebrated, and the weakening of western religious power has done nothing to decrease the gap between rich and poor.

What I found most inspiring in India was the ability of

millions of human beings living on top of each other to be civil. On the journey into central Mumbai I witnessed humanity squashed between highway and railway. Narrow homes of cloth and tin sheltered thousands of people. I saw sick and dying, pregnant and young crowded together in a thin ribbon of life between the tracks and the tarmac. Dust and rubbish blew in the wind but the houses were kept clean. I observed a tall woman in her colourful sari wash her hair under a bucket. Shaking the water from her hair she stood proud.

I looked down from bridges onto streets of pedestrians swarming with thousands of people all moving in the same direction. On foot later, I plunged into the tide of one of these one-way malls and was swept along for several blocks before cutting down an alley and finding the reverse flow to bring me back. I was a cork in an ocean of humanity and the sea was calm. I felt no aggression, saw no disputes or conflicts.

I was confused by what I was observing. Individuals in western democracies would not tolerate the living conditions of the poor of India. There would be revolution, insurrection. Hinduism allowed the horrors of the caste system, the burning of wives and exploitation of children. It also promoted a calm acceptance that allows a billion people to coexist in chaotic harmony. And this national religion was not anti-science. The Indians build their own computers, space rockets and telecommunication systems. Despite a growing taste for Coca-Cola, American culture is largely held at bay. The hit records and movies and books are Indian. I wasn't sure if I liked the effects of a strong national religion or if they scared me. I kept my eyes open for manifestations of the religious.

One day in Kerala I watched women bring Trivandrum City to a standstill. For days their men had been invading the town carrying statues of female deities on their heads, blocking roads with their bulky brightness and ears with their clanging drums and cymbals. Now the women stream in, thousands upon thousands of sari clad women filling up the centre of the city and spilling out as they scramble for a tiny plot on which to build a fire. For a few coins they buy a clay pot and three or five bricks. They queue for water from a fire truck.

Deep in the bowels of a great temple, priests are performing rites to the explosive rhythms of drums and the drones of a choir. Throughout the morning they have been busy awakening the deities and fussing over them, making promises and sacrifices, purifying with smoke and water and with long pure notes. Inside the tempo quickens, outside the women squat and settle. A priest lights the first fire. The flame is shared, is passed along the line of women and out of the temple, multiplying outwards in geometrical progression. One, two, four, eight, sixteen fires.

Coconut-husk kindling bursts into flames as ten thousand pots are set on ten thousand fires. Heating water slowly tosses grains of rice into lazy somersaults, quickening, shimmering, simmering, bubbling, boiling. Steaming pots of rice in coconut milk, of lentil stew and pulse broths. Rolls of proto-sugar jaggery and coconut rice lie like wholesome dog turds on banana leaf plates. Smoke and spice and all things nice. Cooked, covered. Lying in wait.

The sun pulls itself high into the humid, smoky sky and forces heat down onto the bowed heads below. Flames and hot bricks bake shins and ankles. Women faint and fall, and are lifted and raced to shade and water until, recovered, they return to their sacred hearths. And wait.

Gradually the priests fan out from the temple, blessing every pot they meet with holy water and showers of flowers. Priests can't multiply like bursting fires, and it takes all afternoon for them to flow away from the temple compound and through the crowded streets and laneways dispensing their blessings.

The women slowly disperse. They carry their precious red clay temple pots, blackened and smoky and blessed. They walk home, or crush onto rust-red buses and hot, hard trains.

All the female-deity temples of Kerala hold their own Pongala. Pongala is also the name for the porridge of jaggery, coconut and plantain, which is apparently the favourite offering to the goddesses. Every local shrine has a day each year when the women come to cook, but the central Attukal Bhagovathy temple draws women from all around the state and fills a square kilometre with patient, fainting, smoke-stained, sun-touched women needing fire trucks to water them.

It seems remarkable that so vast an outpouring of religious faith still occurs in a modern world. More so to realise that this massive response is not an ancient tradition. It has been going for sixty years, seventy at most. Why? What draws housewives and nurses, teachers and doctors, dancers and rocket engineers, mothers and daughters, good women and bad to these streets surrounding this temple? Why is Trivandrum brought to a standstill?

Daksha, a dance guru from the north, believes it is just a clever marketing ploy of the temple priests. With every woman donating a few coins it is their biggest payday. She blames economic rationalism for this irrational behaviour. I prefer to believe the myth I heard …

Back in time when kings and princes ruled and people knew their places — the poorest untouchable, the richest unseeable — there lived a couple of dancers. Husband and wife, they plied their exquisite trade around the temples and courts, sinuous bodies and stamping feet reflected in oil lamp glare. Oh they were very good, but they couldn't make a living. Their names were Kovilan and Kannaki, and they starved because of honour. A hard, ragged virtue–reality.

Kannaki was chaste to a fault. She would countenance no man except her husband, the partner of her dance. In those olden days, not so very long ago, the temple dancers were also courtesans. They seduced their patrons with the mystery and verve of their bodies and later satisfied them with the touch of their flesh. It was accepted. It was expected. Kannaki would dance magnificently, spin her beautiful body with a promise of passion and stamp her naked, bell-encrusted feet with such a powerfully precise climax that princes squirmed and bulged in anticipation. But then she spurned them, refused their mighty members and clung chastely to her husband. A right royal cock-teaser.

She naturally received only a pittance for her efforts and an empty belly for her pride. Eventually the couple was destitute. Their ribs began to show and their dance began to suffer. Kovilan felt powerless and despaired.

He watched quietly one morning as his beautiful wife dressed in her finery and danced alone, just for the sake of the dance. Her exquisite costumes, handed down through her family, lay scattered on the ground, memoirs of the prosperous times gone by. Perhaps her grandmothers had been happy to spread their legs for kings. For the silks, gold and silver threads and gems were, albeit now tattered and tarnished, of the finest quality.

Kovilan saw a wife so thin her bangles slid off. He marvelled that she could yet dance strongly enough to transform into the goddess. He knew she would not be dancing much longer. In hungry desperation and the despair of seeing his lovely wife suffer, Kovilan took one of her silver anklets to the market to sell.

He hoped she might not miss it, but knew she would. It was a curved and hollow silver tube, filled with things that tinkled, decorated in swirly details. He attracted notice as he tried to hawk his heirloom, and in his ragged clothes was taken for a thief. Police (or soldiers, or whatever they used to catch criminals then) roughly grabbed the poor man and bundled him away.

'I am not a thief!' he cried to innocent bystanders and inquisitive passers-by.

'The anklet is my wife's,' he pleaded to the uncaring wallopers who dragged him through the crowds. He repeated it to sergeants and guards.

'My wife is Kannaki, the famous court dancer. I am trying to sell her anklet that she might eat,' he pleaded to the magistrate. The magistrate had been a fan of Kannaki, and could not believe this scrawny wretch could be married to so magnificent a beast. He condemned Kovilan to death.

'The king,' shouted Kovilan, the fear of death giving him sudden courage. 'I demand my right to be put before the king. He will know me. I have danced with my wife many times before the Maharaja. The king will set me free.'

On the slight possibility that this filthy madman was important to his boss, the magistrate allowed Kovilan the ancient right of audience. The king looked down and saw dirty hair, a distended stomach and a limping, battered body (the police had not held back). It did not stir any memories of liquid dance. 'Off with his head!' he cried.

Word got back to Kannaki, who raced to the palace as fast as hungry legs can hurry. She reached the courtyard at the very moment her beloved husband's head hit the polished tiles. One dull and dreadful drumbeat of bone on stone.

As blood spurted from the only neck she would ever kiss Kannaki walked tall towards the king, her shock and loss empowering her, enlarging her. She pulled a second anklet from beneath her sari and demanded the king compare it with the first. Yes, it was the same as the one the beheaded thief had stolen.

'Open one of them,' she demanded of her ruler. He stared at her blankly.

'Open it!' she spat. 'Inside you will find precious jewels. I know that because they are mine. Open it and see that the man you have killed was innocent.'

The guards had surrounded Kannaki by now, but the king waved them away. He was intrigued. Nothing this interesting had happened for weeks. This angry apparition spattered in her husband's blood captivated him. He called for a sword, and smashed the blade down onto the hollow circle of silver. Rubies and diamonds spilt out onto the floor. The king was amazed. He had no idea that the lovely bell-like ankle music was made from this.

'Pardon him!' ordered Kannaki. 'Admit you were wrong and that a great injustice has been done!'

Kings don't admit publicly to mistakes. He smirked at her.

'How could I have known what lay within them but that the anklets are mine, along with the knowledge of their making?'

The king had no answer.

'My husband is an innocent man. He shall not die in shame. Stand now and declare that you were wrong and that he was an honourable man!'

The Maharaja must have know she told the truth but he could not reply, could not admit, could not rescind. He could as easily put back the head as say sorry. It was against his kingly nature.

Kannaki waited. The court, the guards and soldiers waited. The gods waited. The king just sat. Absolute power sat powerless before the steel fury of a righteous woman. He was impotent and slack. He shook his head and denied her.

With a strength that must have been god-given, Kannaki danced one last time. A flashing dance of hands which quickly pulled her sari from her shoulders. A flash of breast revealed. The very breasts this very king had once desired. This time he got them.

Her dancer's fingers with her courtly nails spun into her flesh. She slashed and dug and ripped her bosom free. She tore off her useless paps, the symbol of desire that had caused all this, and threw them into the unbelieving face of the king.

Bleeding from her ghastly wounds she glided across the flagstones like a dancer, paused briefly to bid her husband farewell, and then walked out through the palace gates. No one moved until her spell was broken.

The king, spluttering and destroyed, demanded she be found and put to death. But she wasn't. Women smuggled her away, out of Tamil country and across a thousand miles of dusty roads. She came at last to Thiruvananthapuram where eventually she died.

This is the Tamil epic of Chillapaphikaram, the god of dance. Kannaki was human, and was god. Her story true, and mythical. They say she was buried at the Attukal Bhagavathy temple. And now, a millennium later, her memory causes tens of thousands of women to bring a city to a standstill.

Why? What has made this story so potent in the last sixty years? It seems to me it is the response of modern Indian women to the theme of women's power — the ancient tale of a common woman who stood up to a king gives encouragement to their struggle for ascendancy in

Indian culture. They are still oppressed, but are determined to grow in strength.

In northern Kerala I watched a Theyyam unfold. Five dancer/actors prepared themselves to become gods. They lay still for five hours as a master painted intricate designs upon their faces. For an hour or more they were dressed by young acolytes who ensured that every hem was straight and their bracelets shone in the sunlight. Huge headdresses of bamboo, cotton and paint were lashed to their shoulders. One performer had silver cataracts fastened to his eyes. One at a time, at intervals staggered throughout the day, each would take their turn in the temple compound. Drums and trumpets heralded their arrival and set up a manic current of noise to guide the god into the man. As the drums beat ever faster the performers opened up their souls and, looking into mirrors, saw themselves as gods. The deity entered a human body and once again lived upon the earth.

Each god in turn danced around the inner temple building, bringing weapons, water, fire, incense, burning leaves and other mystical objects to the priests and their altars. A young man in white followed them, a large jug of water balanced on his head. As he danced to the drums the water spilled down upon him, wetting his clothes thoroughly and revealing his humanity. The gods turned and spun, a chicken was sacrificed and young men ran across hot coals. The sun beat down upon us and magic ruled the world.

Eventually each god faltered to a halt, his duty and his battery finished. Part human again, he wandered the crowd accepting coins and blessing each donation with pats of powdered spice. I chose the monkey god to bless me, for his energy and humour best matched mine. As he came close and placed his hand upon my head I saw again the intricacies of his painted face. From even a small distance he just looked green. I asked one of the master painters why the patterns, applied with such care, were of a design such that they were invisible from more than a few feet.

'We do not paint for the pleasure of your eyes,' he told me. 'The work is for the gods. They know the care we take and understand the skill and sacrifice. We paint this beauty for them. They see it, and they come.'

On the way back to town in a taxi I saw a god dancing amongst the rusting hulks of broken trucks. Our driver stopped and reversed for me to see the dancing deity, and the villagers ran to the car and dragged us out and into the fray. As luck would have it, the arrival of strangers was auspicious for this ritual of the blessing of the trucks, and we were enticed to stay with sweet coconut wine. This god, who danced with gay abandon and giant yellow lips, called me to him for a blessing. He laughed as he dusted me with yellow rice and wished me a good life. My whole soul beamed back happiness. It is a lovely thing, being blessed.

It had taken me a long time to get to the subcontinent, home to 3.3 million gods. Poppa Doiki's homily on the five stages of man had kept me from chasing gurus while I was still young and anyway I had always been more interested in the spirit of Australia. But now I had a reason to visit I plunged into India — and I felt refreshed. The gods dance in the temples and in truck stops and touch you with their hands. You do not need faith to see these gods; other people bring them forth. You can deny them and see only masked performers if you wish, but if you allow them, and stand in the sun long enough, you feel the truth of a grand existence.

The End of Magic

Back home from India my work sent me to another magic land — the Kimberley. From the land of the sacred cow to cattle country.

I was working with two award-winning actors — Ningali Lawford (a traditional woman from the Kimberley) and Kelton Pell (a Nyoongar actor from Perth) — rehearsing a play we had been writing over the previous year. Two blackfellas and one white, two men and one woman, a collaboration of three. Through united vision, trust and mutual respect we developed ways to write together. The play, *Solid*, is about Aboriginal people from different places (the north and the south), and different cultures (traditional and urban). It examines what culture is, and why there is enmity between the tribes. It is passionate, funny, angry and sad.

We rehearsed on Kupardiya Station, a hundred kilometres south-east of Fitzroy Crossing. Leased and run by Ningali's family, the cattle station is an all blackfella concern which exports beef to Japan. It is an ancient land of endless plains across which sprawls a mighty river with beautiful deep pools of clear water. The vast majority of people in the Fitzroy Valley are Aboriginal. They live in towns, on stations and in isolated communities. Big mob of blackfella, as they say.

There were lots of interruptions, and a four-day sandstorm that was really unpleasant. Eventually we made a windproof theatre out of an unused shed and started performing, taking the play to a number of communities up the valley as we journeyed towards Broome and the coast. We saw some awesome places, and strong and proud communities planted amongst towering ridges. The people (not all, but a lot) seem to be thriving again, contrary to the predominant images people have of Aboriginal communities — the images of despair chosen by the media. Whilst there are huge problems that need solving I have witnessed many happy communities. It was my privilege to be invited into isolated out-stations, to see how the people are re-establishing cultural life.

Wherever we performed there would be a hundred kids at the front with a pack of dogs (and even a pig at one place). The older people tended to stay back in the darkness. They listened and enjoyed the show and found it valuable. Nyoongar and Kimberley people have been traditional enemies, and early governments exploited this enmity by using north-west blackfellas as police-aids in the south and Nyoongars in the north. The older people thought that it was important that their communities understand the trials of their brothers in the south. They were pleased to hear Nyoongar stories and were glad our play communicated a message of unity. They believed that was the way forward.

One night, behind a dilapidated shack at the back end of Fitzroy Crossing, we were introduced to two old ladies who shared stories with us. As they talked about their childhood, an old man came out of the house to join us. He became agitated as the sisters told more stories. He kept telling me that he also had yarns to tell but he couldn't get a word in. His sisters ruled the airwaves. He sat in frustration until I was able to grab a silence and throw the focus to him. A group of young men who had been sitting around another fire moved over to hear his words. He was a mumban man, a magic man and healer.

He told of being taken by a dingo as a baby, and showed us his chest scars to prove it. Apparently he was picked up so gently by the beast that he quietly gurgled as it carried him out of the camp. Only when the wild dog had him alone in the creek bed some distance away, did it start to tear at his flesh. The infant screamed loudly and his people came running to find him covered in blood. Some counselled to let him die. Living in a fragile balance in the bush, an injured baby would hold them up, deplete their resources and threaten their survival. Others argued for the child's life. Despite his terrible injuries he was still crying loudly and demanding his right to live a full life. Such was the strength of his cry that his call was heeded. He lived.

He grew. He trained and became mumban man, a healer. The scars on his chest marked him for a special role. Various men around the circle offered me instances of healing and magic that the old fella had accomplished. They did not expect a white man to take such things seriously, yet very much wanted me to believe. They were not to know I had a Niuginian father who was a shaman and that I had a healthy respect for the weird. And while I don't automatically accept every claim of power and spirit life I hear, this old fella's wicked scars and open eager eyes convinced me of his story.

I asked the old man if his knowledge would die with him. He looked up very sharply and asked what I meant. I asked if he was training anyone to take over when he was gone. He smiled and looked around the motley group who sat at his feet.

'Where could I find a young man with the patience these days?'

One long-limbed bloke sheepishly lifted an arm and looked intently at the old man. The old fella laughed back at him.

'None of you could sit still, none of you could listen without questions, none of you could give up the grog.'

'I could,' pleaded the tall young man.

'Not for year after year! It's gone now. All finished now. You got hospitals now, and television, and grog. What you need my old stuff for?'

The tall young man quivered next to me, saddened to his bones. Later that night he travelled east with us for an hour or two. His conversation was erudite and witty. He had studied western law for a number of years until the inhuman litany of torts and contracts wore him down. He wanted to be a lawman, but the white law was too removed from his experience, and the black law was dying. I never saw him again, but still feel that this languid lanky cowboy had the talents and vision that his people require — the ability to become a bridge between the old law and the new, the old generation and his own. Unfortunately, there is no recognised career or training path for such people and I fear he is likely to give up and sit unmoving and uninspired in the sand.

That night I sat beside our camp fire feeling terribly sad. It seemed that I had witnessed a symbolic ending of an ancient line, the night an old man spoke to deny a successor. All the world's ancient ways were on the edge of annihilation, and I had heard one of the branches snap.

The next day we had a long drive, and I lay in the rear of the troop carrier and watched the Kimberley flow past the window. A landscape unchanged for a million years since the seas retracted leaving ancient coral ridges. Fat boab trees reached out their stumpy limbs. Sunlight and breeze created flashing patterns in the coolabah leaves. I pondered on endless streams of time, on the end of streams of knowledge; mumban men and the ancients. I decided that I did believe in magic, even if I was too cautious to play with it myself.

It seemed to me, as I sped along the grey-blue ribbon that crossed the deep red earth, that perhaps the physical realm we inhabit, with all its laws of physics, is only a possibility that we have made concrete to ensure our survival. We grow up believing in the solidity of the earth and its immutability. Without this sense of the solid we could not exist as we do, the earth could not have evolved as it has. But reality could not be as solid as it seemed. Poppa Doiki sailed through the ether to Melbourne.

Gurus and elders from around the world preach of different realities. Even our modern physicists speak of twelve dimensions and parallel universes, and wormhole distortions in time and space. Everything and nothing exists. It is all space and possibility; endless, timeless nothingness brought into being by awareness. He who is aware is a god. Together we are such powerful gods that we form the world out of nothingness. The aware can go anywhere, be anything: transmute into animal spirit, bound across the desert, stand on red-hot rocks, and levitate. The laws of nature are only a convenience that living creatures, spirits and gods have allowed/developed to give us a terra firma on which to thrive. We can break the laws, like all laws, when we truly believe them to be arbitrary. Or so it seemed that afternoon.

I wanted to see if I could test this, and decided to allow myself to believe it. Lying back on my swag I watched the scrub rush past. I imagined the space between the trees, between the molecules, between the quantum particles. I allowed the solidness of our collective fantasy to dissipate. And it did. I soared through the steel and glass walls of the vehicle and moved through the trees. I seemed to ride a wave that lifted me gently above the dry, grey scrub and then tilted me down into and through the solid trunks. Everything began to part, the molecules of my body and the wood of the trees, as I swept through bark and swooped towards the dirt. I think I was terrified, but so in awe of the adventure that the fear never had a chance to stop me.

'What the fuck is he doing here?' demanded Kelton, sweeping my attention back into my body and the car. I grabbed hold of a window to pull myself safely back into the land of the solid. And looking out I saw a middle-aged white man walking purposely along the roadside.

We all cheered and stared. What was a whitefella doing out here all alone, fifty kilometres from the nearest town, well dressed and striding with apparent purpose. Should we stop and rescue him? Kelton, the driver, insisted the bloke had waved that he was okay. We speculated. He wasn't carrying a petrol can, or a backpack, or water. We had passed no broken-down vehicles or turn-offs to stations. He didn't look like a Japanese endurance nut or a millennium survivalist out to find God in the desert. He looked surprisingly suburban, and weirdly out of place.

I began to laugh, and then tried to explain my experience to the others. For the first time in my life I was flying through matter, time and space, only to be brought suddenly back to solid reality by the manifestation of a suburban man walking in the middle of nowhere. The coincidence of these two bizarre experiences occurring together was too weird to contemplate. He was the only person we had seen walking the Kimberley roads in a month of travel. Had he appeared at the right second to pull me back from the brink? It was equally bizarre that we didn't stop to check up on him. It is natural behaviour, expected behaviour in Australia's vast arid lands, to stop and help lost strangers in need. Yet Kelton was sure the man neither needed nor wanted us to stop, and nobody questioned his perception. We all accepted that the man was supposed to be there, calmly walking into the vastness.

It could have been coincidence, but it seemed to me that something, or someone, didn't think it wise for me to go swooping through the ether alone without guide, maps or compass. I had slipped into my flight of fancy with such ease that I hadn't thought about the consequences of getting lost. Astral travelling from the back of a speeding vehicle may well be an exceedingly dangerous and stupid thing for a novice to do. Had I continued to fly through the earth before deciding to return to my flesh, my body may have been far from where I left it. I fancied the wandering man was some sort of guardian rescuing me from my adventurous stupidity, or perhaps a manifestation of the spirits of that ancient land come to chase the naive white-spirit away in a form that would not scare.

Millennium

Late in 1999 I took Nina south to visit my uncle and, one afternoon when she was playing on his computer, I went for a walk. I was wearing the blue lightning thongs, long stripped of magic by my simply not believing any more. I walked into the bush on the other side of the street and found a granite outcrop surrounded by the tops of trees, which looked down into the heart of the town. I could see pedestrians and dogs, but they couldn't see me.

I sat on the granite and looked across the harbour. Birds swooped and fell and danced around me. The modern town below looked insubstantial, as if it had been formed with papier-mâché and painted onto the ancient rocks. Time stretched out before me. For the first time I turned my thoughts to the coming of a new millennium. I had been trying to ignore the hype. It was just a bunch of arbitrary numbers turning over into zeroes. That afternoon I pondered on the power of the human imagination and realised that the millennium switchover could indeed be significant for those who allowed it to be.

I began to think about the last thousand years of human endeavour. What had we achieved? I realised with a start that as a species we could claim, at the end of this particular thousand-year cycle, to have dominated our habitat planet. A century ago we couldn't do it, but by the end of the twentieth century mankind could live anywhere on earth. There is no niche, except the deepest ocean trenches and craters of live volcanos, where we cannot survive if we want to. The planet is finally, completely, ours. Which leads to the inevitable question: now that we have won it, what do we want to do with it?

This is *the* question for the new millennium. Now that we own the planet, what are we going to do with it? If we assume that species domination of habitat is an underlying natural imperative, what does the species do when it has reached its target? Overpopulate and die? Do we want to manipulate nature so as to allow as many humans as absolutely possible to live on the planet? Do we want to retain climatic and geographic variation, or shall we attempt to homogenise everything for the sake of efficiency? Do we want just one dominant culture, or a myriad of possibilities? Shall we protect what few sacred places remain, or does the brave new world do away with magic?

With our ability to flatten forests and eat mountains, we have the means to close all the gateways and finish with sorcery. But I'm not at all sure that is a good idea. I think we lose a great deal of human potential if we restrict the worlds in which we play. Our spirits will be the poorer.

I treasure the moments of magic in my life, and I felt that I was ready, sitting on that granite hilltop as we rapidly approached a cusp of history, to declare my hand and share my stories. I had an overwhelming desire to bring this book into the world, and an urge to do it soon. In fact I wanted to finish it by the end of the year. No, that wasn't quite it, it wasn't exactly my want. It was more that I felt compelled to finish the bastard. I blame the thongs, although it may have been the granite on which I sat. Perhaps I had unconsciously found a gateway in the bush. Whatever the cause, I sensed I was not alone. I felt as if Popeye PK and Poppa Doiki were around me, urging me on. 'Finish it son,' ran the words in my head.

What a terrible vision! If I was going to get some sort of message I would rather it were something more uplifting than an exhortation to finish writing by a certain date. It was embarrassing. I had been throwing cold water on the whole millennium industry for years. But now I had to take it seriously. I hated the vision, but it was so strong, so unexpected, so unlike what visions are supposed to be that I believed it. When I got home I began to write like a man possessed.

When I stopped and read over the first chapter, I was left wondering how it could possibly have happened like that. I felt at times that I was reading a Boy's Own adventure story. Plucky white boy disarms drunken ruffians, negotiates snakes and overcomes injury to find a magic cave and an old magician. I felt nauseated. I soon realised that this was a difficulty I had to deal with. Essentially the story of the breathing cave was true. I couldn't rewrite it to make it less classical. It happened the way it did. I had simply gone north to perform a play and stumbled into something rich. That it unfolded as it did is part of the mystery.

Many of the other stories I have told were just as unlikely and paint me as having led a charmed life. I realised I could not afford to get worried each time this cropped up. All I could do was tell the stories as they happened, and keep my humour. As the time ran out even my subconscious was getting edgy. I started waking at five am and jumping straight into the writing.

As I edited my New Guinea journeys I found it hard to

believe that I had been able to so easily put such dramatic experiences to one side and get on with secular life. The memory of the red light at Oropot still brings goosebumps, yet somehow the young man who was me was able to put aside such terrifying happenings and pretend that the world was as solid and normal as he had been taught. I guess that is what most of us do when facing the inexplicable. It was possible then for me to forget these things, to bury the weird and carry on regardless. Yet strange things continued happening in my life. I didn't chase the gurus, but perhaps something was chasing me. I had been so cynical about the year 2000 yet now I had a dose of millennial madness of my own. I had to finish the book before it drove me mad. I wrote day and night. I ate badly and ignored friends, and missed all the parties of the silly season.

I slept little the night before New Year's Eve, and was up at dawn hammering away. It was the middle of a heatwave and by midday the sweat was dropping on the keys. I napped briefly, then renewed my fevered writing. By early evening I had finished the editing and rewriting to my satisfaction, except for the last chapter. I was very tired by now, but a strange energy possessed me as I made sense of my life. I found myself on a curve of inspiration that led to midnight. I could see how the story would wind up as the clocks struck and the fireworks exploded. I was going to succeed. I would finish the story a little after midnight, the first book of the year 2000. In my manic exhaustion I fantasised about international publishers being captivated by the first book of Y2K.

I reached the last few pages a little ahead of myself and decided to run the spell-check through the document. It took longer than I thought. I was still re-arranging grammar and spelling when I heard fireworks over the city. My computer clock agreed that it was midnight. Time to stop the checking and write my final paragraphs and finish the book.

Outside a flash and a rumble. Not fireworks, but thunder. I searched my brain for the final words. I was too tired to remember properly what I had wanted to say. As I was reaching inside for inspiration there was another flash of lightning. And the lights and my computer flickered for a mini-second.

On/off/on!

And I lost it all. I could find nothing on my auto-save. In my tiredness and desperation I had neglected to save my writing since mid afternoon. Now it had gone into cyberspace. I was devastated. How could I have been so stupid? For years we had been warned of the Y2K bug on this very night, of the risk of computer failure and power loss at midnight, and I had sailed through the evening without the slightest precaution. I felt like an idiot. The irony that it was old-fashioned lightning, rather than Y2K, that had destroyed my work was of no comfort. I felt awful. I hated myself. The whole frantic project to finish the work that night seemed to be such a fraud I felt like crying. So much for the vision. It was all fucking nonsense and I wanted to die.

I found the strength to shut everything off and get in my car. I drove out of town and down long roads through dark bush to reach a party to which I had been invited. I didn't really feel like partying, but I couldn't stay in the house. It had been my prison for weeks and I was too stir crazy to remain. I might have done something stupid like destroy the computer and lose the entire work.

I felt like a ball of tightly knotted wire. I hated my stupidity. I wished I had gone south with my kids for a holiday rather than insisting on staying in a hot house to finish a stupid book. I missed them, and resented the sacrifice I had made.

But then I came to realise that I had still made the sacrifice the vision had demanded. I had worked my bum off staring cross-eyed at a screen. I had faced my life and the peculiar irrational incidents that populated it, and made some sort of sense of it, to me at least. I had done the hard work that had been asked of me.

The lightning flash loss was probably a godsend. I sensed that during those last tired hours I had written badly. I had been so busy congratulating myself on my victory over time that I wasn't taking the work itself very seriously. In fact I had come to some pretty outrageous conclusions. If I had finished the book just after midnight, logged and dated it as proof and sent it away to publishers I could have been very embarrassed. Better, perhaps, to be forced to have another look in the clear light of day.

The loss was as significant as I wished to allow it to be. I could choose to never finish the book now, or I could use that moment of acute stupidity as a self-deprecating finish to my story. I could even take the story a little further, and into the party celebrating the new century.

I drove up a long driveway and was nearly bogged in deep sand. I walked down a dirt track to the house, where I found grass lawns leading down to a well-lit stage. A band was rocking and rolling and people danced. Towards the back I found an old friend over from Sydney. It was Christine, the woman who had called me to Lancelin where we ran into sea eagles. She was the last person I expected to see. I briefly described the tragedy of my evening. I told her this party was now essential to the fate of my book. If I had a good time there would be a happy ending. If I went home feeling like shit I had a gloomy tome on my hands.

Christine borrowed a saxophone and joined the band on stage. I danced with friends beneath the Southern Cross. I danced out all my anger at myself; I danced the joy of new beginnings. I marvelled at the stars and at the simple joy of music, friends and dance. Life was good.

I wandered up a firebreak through the bush. The music was still clear. Away from the lights the stars were vivid. I lay in the dirt and watched the stars slowly turn.

'Is that it?' I wondered. 'Is the magic of music and stars enough for me now? Can I settle down to normal life?' I listened to the music and the gentle breeze. Deep down, below the other sounds, I hear something else. Unearthly, but from the earth. Breath.

Slowly in — silence — slowly out — silence — slowly in —

'Final Chapter'

This morning I walked part of the way up a mountain on which a god lives. At least that is what the sign explained at the base of Western Australia's second highest mountain. The massive fractured spine of iron ore slabs certainly looked awesome enough to house a god or two. The violently angled ridges dominated an already extraordinary landscape. This was Karijini National Park, deep in the Pilbara, a thousand kilometres north-east of Perth.

I am in Tom Price conducting drama workshops and setting up another tour of *Bidenjarreb Pinjarra*, the comedy about a massacre. Today I was free after eleven am and drove into the mountains. I should really have been ensconced in my room finalising this book. It was recently returned from my editor, and I am behind schedule in the rewrites.

The editor assigned by my publisher is none other than the woman who travelled with me to Europe many years ago. The Janet who was with me when I climbed Glastonbury Tor and when I met tribal people for the first time. I have had very little contact with her in the twenty-one years since we split up, and for Janet to be chosen seemed a most unlikely coincidence. I was not at all sure if I was happy with the choice until we met and discussed things. When she returned my manuscript I was unsure again. Virtually every page was painted with codes and queries. I had to re-read the text carefully and craft hundreds of changes. Generally her suggestions were excellent and effecting the changes was merely time consuming. However her big questions about my objectives were most challenging, and had held me up. I borrowed a laptop computer and headed north, promising to have my manuscript completed on return.

As I drove through the spinifex scrub this morning I thought deeply about my intentions with this book. I pulled off the road and up a track to a lookout. On a parapet above the highway a sacred place had been created. A number of rocks had been painted and turned into a shrine, with dried flowers and toys for a lost father and friend. I MISS YOU DAD. I LOVE YOU. I felt the tenderness and tenuousness of human existence. Sympathetic grief stirred deep within my belly and tears spilled, as I tasted a little of the emotions that had been shed and shared in this wild place.

As I drove further into the wilderness I thought about the sacred. It is important to most humans to have places where we can commemorate loss and overcome the miseries of existence. I had just visited a modern shrine, built out of chips of iron ore and plastic objects on a small corner of a vast foreign country. I have no idea why the shrine was built there on a lookout in the middle of nowhere, but it obviously served a deep need and resonated with power.

At the base of Punurrunha, Mount Bruce, is a sign that describes the importance of this striking mountain to the local blackfellas, the Kurrama people. It tells the story of the time when the earth was soft and five young women enticed three men into the sky to form what we know as the saucepan in the stars. Central to the tale is the idea of a god, Minigala, who lived within the peak of Punurrunha watching over the people and places of this culturally rich land. I started walking with a sense of expectation. This very week I had to finalise my book and here I was climbing the slopes of another sacred rock. The cycles seemed close to completion. The universe had conspired to bring me here in a time of need.

I sat under the shade of a coolibah tree. No bullshit, that is exactly where I sat as I stared at the peak and the gorges and vistas which surrounded me. On this side of the ridge I couldn't see the giant slice of land being gobbled up by the nearby Marandoo Mine, or hear the trains and trucks which serviced it. Here things might not have changed for a million years. The flies left me alone as I sat in wonder.

I was wondering about my book. It was time to answer the deeper questions asked by Janet. What was the underlying truth of my experiences, and what was the intention of my text? Under the unmoving gaze of the god of the mountain I made my choices. What you have read up until now has been filtered through the answers that I gave myself this afternoon.

I remembered the pact I had made with a cloud in PNG, that if the shape of Malabo would return I would believe in him. The pact had not been broken. I do believe in spirits.

Despite the iron strength of the red rocks on which I sat I felt once more the insubstantiality of matter. I knew now that it was possible, as I had discovered in the Kimberley, to slide through molecules. From Poppa Doiki I could have learned to fly through space, as once I had, momentarily, with my thongs. I could have defeated the laws of physics and rational thought and travelled through the void if I had chosen that path. I didn't, and I can't, but I do believe I could have.

I confirmed my belief in red-flickering demons that can track down murderers, and caves that breathe and men who can take on the guise of fireflies. I affirmed that a wind spirit had warned me to beware a stranger and that I had seen dancers become gods. All of these things exist in my world. I realise that to admit these things in print is to open myself to ridicule. Yet I have chosen to do just that. Sitting on the rocky slope I understood the book I needed to complete.

The universe laughs at our attempts to define it in merely western scientific terms. Ours is the only culture that is committed entirely to the physical as an explanation for everything. All other cultures, vanished and surviving, have enriched their physical sciences with an understanding of the spiritual world. I believe it is a mark of our arrogance that we disregard all other human constructs of the universe.

It is, of course, fairly common for cultures and religions to believe that their world view is the correct one. What makes our contemporary beliefs especially dangerous is the power we have forged with our rapacious and successful technology. Modern secular science is close to dominating the planet. The most intelligent students in every country are weaned from traditional understanding onto a diet of scientific certainty. The shaman and the priest are treated like idiots and lose their power in the fog of disrespect.

Of course this is not all bad. Much evil has been done in the name of religion. Sorcery can create lifelong fears and protect rascals. Much magic in the world is based on trickery, and many people's lives continue to be ruined by expensive false promises from spiritual charlatans. Science has made modern life a wonderful experience for a lot of westerners. In medicine, transport and communication our lives are transformed, and a great deal of the progress is good for our bodies and souls.

I am not anti-science or pro-spiritual or besotted by animist tribes. I see good and bad in all human cultures. What concerns me is the dominance of the scientist hegemony. I fear that human potential is diminished by the loss of ancient knowledge. I fear that our knowledge of the other will be lost, and our ability to discover new worlds within our own will disappear with the last of the shamans.

Unless we allow that other possibilities exist we condemn other ways to ridicule. Even the world's 'great' religions become childish through scientific gaze. Such a dismissive gaze overturns all the ways we humans have learned to live with each other over the millennia. For thousands of years it has been the love of the gods and the fear of divine retribution which has cemented civil order. The brave new world of science and technology depends on an overworked police force to hold evil in check. To disregard all belief in the mysterious is cruel and dangerous. It condemns everyone to finding happiness within a finite life span and robs us of solace when we lose our loved ones.

In Australia the prevailing denial of spiritual matters has important social ramifications. We face a major social decision about our treatment of Aboriginal people. Left unchecked it will blow up in our faces. Blackfellas are growing in numbers and strength and one day the anger will boil over. Unresolved, the Aboriginal 'problem' remains both a ticking time bomb and a major object of international criticism, eating away at our national dignity and self-respect. Land and cultural rights are fundamental in any attempt to right past wrongs and allow our indigenous people to thrive into the future. However, land rights will never be given by a nation which has no belief in the possibility that the land has a spiritual dimension.

For Aboriginal people to achieve functional equality in their own country they need to be able to practise their beliefs. We newcomers have brought our own churches and science, but sneer at the 'primitive' beliefs of the old people. We must allow blackfellas the dignity of their spiritual knowledge. That spiritual knowledge requires continual access to powerful land, which in itself requires whitefellas to accept that land has power. That is a long and difficult journey for us to make in the glare of our disbelieving science.

Popeye PK once interpreted the breathing cave as a message to me that the spirits still live. Such knowledge has enabled me to cross cultural barriers, to accept other people for what they are, to respect them whatever their beliefs may be. This openness has in turn brought me more demonstrations of the power and mystery of life on this planet. It has been a rich journey, full of privileged insight and high adventure.

I have written this book to help keep the possibilities alive, and to encourage open minds. When we remove the blinkers of certainty we can mingle more easily with others. Next time you wander in the bush take a few steps off the track and sit under a tree. Let time fall away, and open your mind to receive the wonders that surround you. I'm not encouraging you to try flying in thongs or see little people. Just enjoy the simple pleasure of finding your place in the universe. Breathe slowly in and slowly out. Allow things to happen. The spirits still live.

Phil Thomson is an actor, director and playwright whose work has taken him throughout Australia and Papua New Guinea. Many of his plays have involved collaborations with indigenous performers and local communities. A former Artistic Director of Deck Chair Theatre (for which he won the Swan Gold Award for Outstanding Theatre Development) he has recently completed a two-year Senior Artist's Fellowship from the Australia Council, which produced (amongst other works) *Solid*, a major hit of the Perth and Brisbane Festivals.

He has toured several productions to Papua New Guinea, and been Executive Director of the Madang Visitors and Cultural Bureau where he established Malabo (the Provincial Theatre Company), ran a museum and piloted a number of cultural tourism projects.

He is currently a resident writer for Black Swan Theatre and regularly performs in *Bidenjarreb Pinjarra*, an improvised comedy about the first massacre of Aboriginal people in Western Australia. He is currently writing the libretto for *Gilgamesh*, an Indian/Australian dance-theatre work.

Phil lives out the back of Fremantle and shares two teenage children. He plays basketball and seems quite normal most of the time. He is expecting his next experience of the paranormal any year now.

Phil Thomson's writing credits include *Round the Bend**, *Fleets of Fortune**, *Wantok, Paddy**, *Home Port**, *Yagan**, *The Last Sanctuary, ... into the Shimmer Heat, Bidenjarreb Pinjarra**, *Wel-le Dan-joo**, *Phil Thomson's Initiation, Stori Bilong Madang, Hearts & Minds**, *Wrecked Dreams, Solid**, *Kidz Breakfast**, *Jungle Fever* and *One Destiny*.

* indicates collaborations with fellow artists.